A TREASURY OF SPORTS HUMOR

No country in the world has as varied a sports program as the United States—or as strong a tradition and reputation for a sense of humor. Baseball, the Great American Game for more than a century, has understandably spawned more looney characters and inspired more zany situations than any other of our sports—but there are also laughs and anecdotes from the worlds of football, basketball, hockey, golf and all the rest. Dozens of legendary and modern sports figures appear in these pages. Some are heroes, some are victims—but all are good for a laugh.

BOOKS BY MILTON J. SHAPIRO

ALL STARS OF THE OUTFIELD

A BEGINNER'S BOOK OF SPORTING GUNS AND HUNTING

BASEBALL'S GREATEST PITCHERS

CHAMPIONS OF THE BAT: Baseball's Greatest Sluggers

THE DAY THEY MADE THE RECORD BOOK

HEROES BEHIND THE MASK: America's Greatest Catchers

HEROES OF THE BULLPEN: Baseball's Greatest Relief Pitchers

JACKIE ROBINSON OF THE BROOKLYN DODGERS

LAUGHS FROM THE DUGOUT

THE PRO QUARTERBACKS

A TREASURY OF SPORTS HUMOR

THE YEAR THEY WON THE MOST VALUABLE PLAYER AWARD

A
Treasury of
Sports
Humor

MILTON J. SHAPIR

Julian Messner
New York

Published by Julian Messner
a division of Simon & Schuster, Inc.
1 West 39th Street, New York, N.Y. 10018

Printed in the United States of America
ISBN 0-671-32503-5 Cloth Trade
Library of Congress Catalog Card No. 75-176383

INTRODUCTION

Ever since Prehistoric Man gathered around the camp-fire to listen to the tales of the Old Storyteller, the art of the anecdote has been a popular one. And even then, the cagey old boy was probably borrowing somebody else's stories, trimming and polishing a bit, and claiming them as his own.

Historians, tracing the origins of legends, stories of the day and humor, have discovered that many of today's jokes are as old as the Roman hills—and maybe even older. From generation to generation the same old stories are told and retold, changed to fit the times and the country and brought forth as alleged originals.

There's nothing devious about this; it is the nature of anecdotal humor.

And that's the way it is with American sports humor. It is by and large anecdotal humor, situation humor ad libbed at the moment of an event. This inadvertent humor is the best kind; it becomes legend as well as humor, and, because it comes to be regarded as such, it lasts for decades and for generations, and indeed much of it will last as long as Hoyt Wilhelm. Maybe longer.

At the same time, a substantial amount of apocryphal story becomes wedged in among the anecdotes that really have a basis in fact. No matter; these bits of apocrypha are just as important as the fact, for they are as much a part of American sports history as the record books. Besides, considering the strange characters who people these stories, they could just as well be true as not. Experts, writers, athletes, historians, fans—just about everyone by now—swear that all the stories that are told are true. And who is there who will deny it? Who would want to?

Furthermore, what difference does it make who told the original story, who the original characters were and when it all happened? It is enough to say that it happened, or *could* have happened, and it could just as well have happened to the athletes in the story as well as to a dozen other kooky characters out of the past or present.

For example, an anecdote in this book about Frankie Frisch and umpire Bill Klem has appeared elsewhere as an argument between Leo Durocher and umpire George Magerkurth. The story is just as funny, no matter who the combatants, and, more to the point, it could easily have happened with either pair.

The same applies to one story involving Joe Namath
—it was once attributed to Johnny Unitas. A Norm Van
Brocklin story has also been told naming Sammy Baugh
as the hero. And so on.

How old is sports humor? Mac Davis, the sports his-
torian, has traced a bit of wit back to a baseball guide
published in 1868. It was a story about the compara-
tively new game of baseball, and it went on to quote an
accidental witness of the game who said, "I can't see what
fun such great big men can find in hitting a little ball with
a big stick and then run away like mad and kick at a
sand bag."

That story, of course, has been retold thousands and
thousand of times, in many shapes and forms, quoting
any number of different observers of the game of baseball.

The author himself last heard the same story in Venice,
Italy, where it was told to him by a waiter in a café at
St. Mark's Square, who claimed that his father had actu-
ally said these words on his return from a trip to America.

So, there we are.

The essential thing is to laugh.

Milton J. Shapiro

TAKE TWO and HIT to RIGHT

It is said that in recent years baseball has been losing ground to professional football as America's most popular spectator sport. However much truth there may be to this in terms of pure statistics, baseball nevertheless remains the Great American Game. It always will be, for a number of very good reasons.

Baseball has a tradition unique in American sports. It is a part of our folk history, and it has its folk heroes. Names like Cobb and Ruth and Gehrig, DiMaggio and Robinson and Mantle, Musial and Williams are enshrined, in their own way, as are the names of our great statesmen and national heroes.

But much more than all that, baseball is the Great American Game because of its cast of characters, which, down through the years, has given so much joy to so many millions, made so many of us laugh and brought a richness and amiability to the American way of life that virtually became the image of America itself.

Baseball always was, and fortunately still is, chock full of "flaky" characters, perhaps better at providing laughs than at providing the hit or the well-pitched game —and loved all the more for it. Everybody gets into the clown act in baseball—players, managers, even the umpires and the fans.

You will meet many of them on these next pages, and, if you didn't believe so before, you may well believe afterwards that, no matter what else is happening in it, baseball remains one of the funniest acts in show business.

Take, for example, the case of Satchel Paige. The venerable Satch was inducted into baseball's Hall of Fame in the summer of 1971. But not completely. The bust and plaque honoring Satchel will be in a separate part of the Cooperstown museum. You see, old Satch, who retired from baseball when he was about 60, or maybe it was 70—well, old Satch put in only four full seasons in the majors, and the rules say a player has to be judged on a ten-year performance.

Satch's trouble was that he got a late start. He barnstormed around the Negro leagues for ages, a fantastic pitcher, but couldn't get into major-league baseball until 1948, a year after Jackie Robinson broke the color line.

Take Two and Hit to Right

Satch had already pitched at least 20 years when Bill Veeck brought him up to the Cleveland Indians. Paige gave his age *then* as 43, but it was more likely 50.

"There's only two people know how old I am," Paige said early in 1971, "Bill Veeck and me. And we ain't telling."

Satchel's age became a standing joke in baseball. His own teammates ribbed him. Satch loved it all, and could exchange quips with the best of them. Once, one of his teammates began needling him. "Hey Satch," the player said, "what kind of pitch was Connie Mack weak on?"

Satch just smiled. Connie Mack, then owner of the Philadelphia Athletics, went back almost to the beginnings of baseball. Quipped Satch, "Son, you know that was a right funny joke the first time I heard it—from Abner Doubleday!"

Satch used to tell this story on himself when players or reporters questioned him about proof of his age.

He went to Mexico once on an exhibition tour, and at the border he was asked for proof of citizenship.

"You got a birth certificate?" asked the border guard. Replied Paige, "Man, what for you want my birth certificate? Everyone knows old Satch was born."

When Veeck brought Satch up for a trial, everybody thought he was crazy, or simply grandstanding by hiring a black man. No matter how good Paige had been in the

17

Negro League, this was the majors, and Paige was between 40 and 50 years old.

Veeck had him pitch batting practice. The first man he faced was Lou Boudreau, the team's playing manager. Lou was leading both leagues in hitting.

But he didn't lay his bat on 19 of the 20 pitches Satch threw him.

Paige started seven games and won six, helping Cleveland win the pennant in a tight race with Boston. Before the first game of the World Series, a writer approached Paige and asked him if he thought he'd start one of the games.

"Nope, ain't likely," said Satch.

"Why not?" asked the sports writer.

"Counter," said Satch.

"What do you mean, 'counter'?" asked the reporter.

"Counter Feller, Bearden, Lemon and Gromek," replied Satch, naming the Indians' starting four.

Someone was always trying to find out Satchel's real age. Said Satchel, when he retired, "They done a lot of investigating, and, to tell the truth, it puzzles me myself. They couldn't find my record down in Mobile, because the jail had burned down and the judge had died. They did a lot of checking on my family and found out I had some relatives 200 years old."

Veeck, who wrote about Paige in his memoirs, said of him: "All our players were given questionnaires to fill out each year. Sometimes Satch would say he was mar-

Take Two and Hit to Right

ried, other times that he wasn't. Every day, though, he was leaving a ticket at the box office for a Mrs. Paige, and every day a different woman picked it up. At last, to get his marital status straightened out for our records, I asked him about this phenomenon.

" 'Well, it's like this,' said Satch. 'I'm not married, but I'm in great demand.' "

Paige's ammunition on the mound consisted of his famous "hesitation" pitch (a tantalizing slow ball) and a real buzzer of a fast ball now and again. Above all, he prided himself on his control. And, from his days in the rough-and-tumble Negro League, he learned how to use the brush-back pitch.

"Know how I'd pitch to you?" he once said to Ernie Banks. "I'd throw you that necktie ball. You can't hit on your back."

He was also an exponent of keeping the ball low and away to the big hitters. Once, a newsman countered by saying the good hitters would lean in and drive the ball to the opposite field.

"Hah!" said Paige. "That's when I take that button off their shirt under their chin. I got a basketful of buttons at home."

He then recounted the day his control was a bit off. "So this batter said to me, 'You took the second button off my shirt!'

"And I told him, 'My control is off. I was aiming at your top button.' "

19

So old Satch will be getting a place in the Hall of Fame. And content he was, too, with a place outside the regular hall. Satch was well used to that kind of treatment.

"I'm proud to be wherever they put me in the Hall of Fame," he said.

But the man who brought him into major-league baseball was not satisfied. Said Bill Veeck, on hearing the news:

"Some dark night I'm going to sneak into Cooperstown and find out where Satchmo's plaque is and put it in the front room, where it belongs."

Yes, baseball is full of wonderful, funny characters. But what distinguishes the sport is that spirit of camaraderie, of intense yet respectful competitiveness, that leads to good-humored banter among so many major leaguers—even among those who by nature are not comics. For example:

When Mayo Smith began touching up his graying hair recently, Gil Hodges called him up and said, "Say, Mayo, are you standing on your head when you get your shoes shined?"

And among teammates, as well. The subject at the time of a player discussion was astrology, and Willie Crawford remarked that he didn't know what sign of the Zodiac applied to him.

Cracked his Dodger buddy Bill Sudakis, "You don't even know Danny Ozark's signs at third base!"

The frenetic nature of baseball, the tension of the game, sometimes makes funnymen out of serious types and turns drama into pure farce. There was a certain game between Detroit and Minnesota. It is the first inning. The first three Tigers single, then Willie Horton hits a home run.

The phone rings in the press box.

"Get Boswell up," says a voice.

"Wha'?"

"I said get Boswell up!"

"Listen, this is the press box. What do you want?"

A silence, then: "This is Ermer. Carl Ermer [Twins' manager]. What's the number of the bullpen?"

When Lou Brock opened his new flower shop a while back, he was paid a visit by sports writer Joe Falls, who demanded to know what Lou knew about flowers.

"I know lots about flowers," said Lou.

"You do, huh?" said Falls, skeptical.

"Sure," insisted Lou. "There's yellow ones . . . and then there's pink ones . . . and see that bunch over there? They're red ones!"

21

The sports writers, too, get into the act and Clif Keane of Boston is one of the prize characters. The ink on his typewriter ribbon is said to be soaked in snake venom. He takes loving pot shots at everybody. One of his best was scored after the Mets won the World Series in 1969.

He wandered into the Met's clubhouse, snarling. "Bushers!" he screamed. "The luckiest team in baseball history! They even gave you the umpires, and it took you five games!"

Someone warned Keane he was liable to get hit by a bat.

"By who?" yelled Clif. "There isn't a guy in here who could hit anything with a bat smaller than a carpet. If one of these bums swung, I wouldn't even have to duck!"

Nothing is safe from the comic-opera aspects of baseball. What happens on a ball field is at times stranger than fiction, funnier than a comedy writer's script for Flip Wilson or "Laugh-In." Who, for example, would have dared invent the following happening?

In the fifth inning of a game between Cocoa and St. Petersburg, in the Florida State League, Bob Gustafson hit the ball to right. At the crack of the bat, Cesar Cedeno, the right fielder, started racing in to the plate, instead of after the ball.

Yelling for time out, Cedeno dragged the umpires out

to his position, and pointed to a six-foot snake that had slithered over to his position!

Shortstop Ray Busse, a native Floridian, identified the snake as harmless and threw it over the fence.

The umpires, meanwhile, got together and decided that Gustafson's hit had been nullified on account of interference by the snake. It was ruled a time-out. So Gustafson had to get up and bat again.

He hit another single to the same spot.

No snakes this time.

Baseball players, the more colorful ones, often use the diamond for a stage, acting and clowning for the crowd. Several later made careers of it, as did Chuck Connors, who did much better in TV ("Branded") than as a first baseman.

On the other hand, David Hartman of TV's "The Bold Ones" keeps on trying to break into baseball. Every spring he works out with the San Francisco Giants. By now it's more for fun than as a serious gesture. Willie Mays once asked him when he had decided to switch ambitions from baseball to acting.

Replied Hartman: "I turned to acting the first time I looked at a curve ball."

To ball players from the small towns, New York remains a wondrous place. Sal Bando's introduction to the

23

Big Town was a short one. He and fellow Arizona State star Rick Monday had just been signed to a contract with the Athletics, and been taken on a tour with the club. They got to New York.

"We decided to take a walk our first night and see what was happening," reported Sal. "On our way to Times Square, we met a guy walking around wearing a Viking costume.

"We turned right around and walked back to our hotel."

George Thomas, an irrepressible comedian, was named player-coach of Boston a couple of years ago, and he promptly announced to the newsmen, "If I'm caught out after the curfew, I'm out in my capacity as a coach, not a player."

George spent a good part of that season in the dugout after he tore the cartilage in his knee. The following spring, before an exhibition game, he met Cincinnati's Johnny Bench, and said to him: "I see we play the same position, only you have it written on your uniform."

It is this person-to-person jockeying that stands out in baseball humor. It has become practically a fine art.

Pitcher Jim McGlothin took a look at Wayne Granger, the skinny reliever of the Redlegs, and said to him:

"Wayne, you're the only man I know who can shower in the barrel of a shotgun."

The exchanges are traditional on all levels, top to bottom. When former Baseball Commissioner Happy Chandler learned that Ford Frick had been elected to the Hall of Fame, he sputtered, "Next thing you know they'll be voting in Charlie McCarthy. He's a dummy, too, you know. All he ever did, for goodness sake, was 'saw logs.' Why, he slept longer in office than Rip Van Winkle!"

Baseball is also filled to overflowing with practical jokers. Whitey Ford had a reputation around the Yankees as a Hallowe'en character ("Trick or Treat"). Once he called the bluff of a rookie pitcher who claimed that the World Series didn't excite him. Before the next game, Whitey got to the park early and put a new baseball in the rookie's locker, the traditional way a manager announces his starting pitcher for the day.

A few minutes after the young pitcher walked in, the Yankees' trainer went to Whitey and said, "You better tell him *you* did that or I'll have to give him a tranquilizer."

The old timers were worst of all. Perhaps it's because they were given a little more leeway to make merry in those days than players are given now. It may well have had something to do with the temper of the times in the country, as well. Then, too, the players themselves were of a different breed from the player of today—less educated, cruder and certainly less sophisticated as businessmen.

The early days of the New York Mets were funny, but they couldn't compare with the storied years of the old Daffy Dodgers and the St. Louis Cardinals "Gas House Gang." Led by Dizzy Dean, the Gas Housers created havoc on the field and off. They were practical jokers of a unique kind.

One day, when things were getting a little dull during a trip to Philadelphia, Diz got hold of Pepper Martin and Heine Schuble, a utility infielder. They decided to liven things up a bit at the conservative Bellevue-Stratford Hotel, where the club was staying. They went to a nearby Army-Navy store and made some purchases.

Shortly afterward, three men in workers' overalls arrived in the hotel dining room. One had a pencil and paper. The others stood about, pointing. In loud voices they began discussing the changes they were going to make. The chandelier would have to go. The walls would be painted green. As the two talked, the third made notes with his pencil. Meanwhile, the confused waiters and a roomful of diners looked on, bewildered.

Then the three men went to the banquet room, where a boys' welfare organization was in the midst of a dignified convention meeting. The man with the pencil and his two henchmen began moving chairs and tables about, totally disregarding the speaker, and finally wound up in a sort of Three Stooges argument.

Martin threw a phony punch at Dean, who threw himself backward over a table, knocking it down. The mock fight, like something out of a Western saloon brawl, went on for several minutes while the delegates watched, aghast. But finally one of them recognized Dean, and the farce was over. With good humor, the speaker insisted that the three men make speeches, and all was forgiven.

Martin in some ways was a worse practical joker than Dean. One night he almost hit manager Frankie Frisch on the head with a bag of water dropped from his hotel window. When Frisch caught up with him, Martin just smiled and apologized. "Gee, Frank," he said, "I'm awful sorry. If you'll forgive me this time, I'll go out there tomorrow and hit a homer and win the game for you."

Which is exactly what Martin did. The Gas House Gang was like that.

Dizzy's favorite target was the press. One day, interviewed separately by a trio of Brooklyn writers, Diz gave them each a different birth date and birthplace and different predictions about how many games he'd win that season.

"I wanted to give them a scoop," he explained. "I didn't want their bosses to get sore at them for having the same story."

A favorite target of practical jokers was Doc Jorgensen, the trainer of the Pittsburgh Pirates. One day a runner slid into second base and was spiked. Out ran the Doc with his little black bag. As he knelt down, he noticed something strange. The player was smiling. Soon enough, Jorgensen found out why.

When he reached into his bag, the only thing he found in it was a ham and cheese sandwich.

Getting back to Dizzy Dean, he was well worth all the space ever devoted to him by baseball writers. And he still rates a special place—a legend unto himself.

Not very long ago Diz was still at it, tossing off the great lines. He was at the Astrodome in Houston, with Judge Roy Hofheinz, and the subject of discussion at the moment was school dropouts.

"I was 40 years before my time," said Diz. "I dropped out of the second grade."

Diz was indeed an untutored son of a sharecropper. When he broke into the big leagues, he began getting so much money that he didn't know what to do with it. He spent it on the wildest things—gave it away, loaned it away. It flowed through his fingers like water. In short order, and for Diz's own good, Cardinals' owner Sam Breadon put him on a dollar-a-day allowance. Every morning Diz was handed a dollar for his day's expenses.

Dizzy went hot under the collar. He began griping that Breadon, who he'd never met, was the stingiest, meanest so-and-so in all of sports, and he, Dizzy Dean, was going to tell the whole world about it.

He was carrying on like that one day in the clubhouse, grousing out loud about Breadon, when he felt a tap on his shoulder. He turned around, and a man said to him, "What's the trouble, son?"

"It's that Breadon feller," Dizzy growled. "He's the meanest darn nickle-nursin' so-and-so ever walked the earth."

"Why?" asked the man. "Doesn't he pay you enough?"

"No!" said Dizzy. "He oughta be givin' me two dollars a day instead of the puny li'l old dollar I get!"

"I see," said the man. "Supposing you come into my office and we'll talk it over. And, by the way, I'm Mr. Breadon."

The Cardinals' owner and the rookie pitcher disappeared into an office, while the players huddled together to speculate on the outcome of the meeting.

"He'll go to the minors sure," said one player.

"Ol' Sam'll run him right out of baseball," said another.

At that the door of Breadon's office burst open, and out came Dizzy, waving a couple of greenbacks over his head.

"Okay, boys!" he shouted. "I got the two bucks!"

Diz mastered most of the hitters, but one who got to him regularly was Bill Terry of the Giants. One afternoon Terry almost broke Dizzy's leg with a line drive through the box. The next time up, Terry sent a line drive buzzing right by the pitcher's ear. And the third time he almost tore off Dizzy's glove with another line shot.

Pepper Martin sauntered over from third base. "Diz," he drawled, "I don't think you're playing Terry deep enough."

Dizzy once bet a teammate he could strike out Vince DiMaggio every time he faced him that afternoon. The first three times DiMaggio did go out on strikes, but on his fourth trip Vince sent a high foul up behind the plate.

Diz yelled to his catcher, "Drop it! Drop it or I'm ruint!"

Obligingly, the catcher dropped the ball. And Diz then burned over strike three to win his bet.

Dizzy used to drive manager Frankie Frisch crazy. One day in Ebbets Field, Frisch was complaining to Casey Stengel, then managing the Dodgers, about his problem children, Dizzy and his brother, Paul. "They're nuts!" said Frisch.

"How many games they win for you this year?" asked Casey.

"Forty-two," said Frankie.

"And you think you got problems?" cracked Casey. "I got two pitchers who're nuts and they *lost* forty-two for me so far this year!"

It was during that very visit to Brooklyn that Frisch called a clubhouse meeting and began going over the Dodger lineup. Every time he'd advise how to pitch to a player, Dean would contradict him.

"Now this Cuccinello," Frisch would say, "nothing but curves. He hits fast balls pretty good."

"That's funny," interrupted Dean. "I never bothered to dish him up a curve yet, and he's still tryin' to get his first loud foul off'n ol' Diz."

So it went—Frisch going down the line giving advice and Dizzy interrupting to say just the opposite. Finally, Dizzy held up his hand.

"This is a silly business, Frank," he said. "I've won 26 games already, and it don't look exactly right for an infielder like you to be tellin' a star like me how I should pitch."

Another time, just before the opening game of the 1934 World Series with the Tigers, Frisch got as far as the second man in the Tiger lineup, Jo-Jo White, when Dizzy interrupted.

"Aw, c'mon, we're wasting time," said Diz. "Everybody

31

knows I'm gonna pitch the first game, with Paul in relief. Paul will pitch the second, with me in relief. I'll pitch the third, and if I need help, Paul'll come in. Then he'll work the fourth game with me in relief."

The meeting adjourned abruptly.

That 1934 World Series, incidentally, was one of the most exciting and hilarious Series on record. Dizzy, as usual, played a starring role. Even earlier than that memorable clubhouse meeting before the opener, he had begun his clowning.

When the Cardinals came out on the field to start warming up, the Tigers were taking hitting practice. In the cage was Hank Greenberg, the Hall of Fame slugger and one of the all-time homer record holders. Diz marched up to the plate, grabbed the bat out of Hank's hands and ordered the pitcher to serve one up. The pitcher threw, and Diz bounced a line drive off the fence.

Returning the bat to Greenberg, he cracked, "That's the way to hit 'em, Moe."

In the fourth game, sitting on the bench, Diz got so excited that he put himself in the game as a pinch runner. Spud Davis was on first base, and before a fuming Frankie Frisch could do anything about it, Diz had raced over to the umpire and declared himself a pinch runner.

Then, when Pepper Martin grounded to second baseman Charley Gehringer, Diz was an easy force. But he went into second base standing up, and shortstop Billy Rogell's relay to first struck him in the forehead, knocking him out.

He was carried off the field unconscious. When he was revived in the clubhouse, his first words were: "They didn't get the double play, did they?"

It was a World Series, too, where an *umpire* was fined. Bill Klem, the senior National League umpire, was fined $50 by Commissioner K. M. Landis for "overripe language" during an argument with Goose Goslin, the Tiger outfielder, in a Detroit hotel lobby.

But the highlight of the whole Series came, appropriately enough, in the finale of the hard-fought seven-game series. It took place in Detroit.

With Diz pitching, the Cardinals opened a commanding lead, and began rubbing it in. The Tiger fans didn't like it, and with bad blood apparent among the players as well, the fans began hooting and booing the Cardinals. They especially began getting on Joe Medwick, the left fielder, after Joe rapped a sixth-inning triple and got into a bumping session with Tiger third baseman Marty Owen.

Medwick then scored on a single, and the Cardinals were breezing home, 9–0, when Medwick took his position in left field afterward.

As soon as he got out there, he was assaulted by a barrage of fruits, vegetables and assorted rubbish by the left-field bleacherites. Fortunately, as a St. Louis sports writer later reported, the fans' control was as bad as the Tiger pitchers' that day, and the missiles missed their mark.

At the height of the barrage, Pepper Martin and center fielder Johnny Orsatti played catch with grapefruit while Medwick, spotting a photographer hovering around looking for a good spot for a shot, pelted him with a tomato.

With the barrage continuing, shortstop Leo Durocher walked out to the battle area, put an arm around Medwick's shoulder and said, "Don't worry, kid. They can't hurt you."

"Oh yeah," said Medwick. "Well we're winning, 9–0, so you play left field and I'll play shortstop."

Leo declined the invitation.

The barrage got so bad, finally, that Commissioner Landis ordered Medwick out of the game for his own protection.

That was baseball in those days, and those were the players.

Later, when Diz retired from baseball—prematurely, owing to an injured shoulder—he turned his colorful gift of gab to the airways. He became a sports announcer, broadcasting the St. Louis baseball games.

In his own Arkansas style, Diz turned the broadcasting world on its ear, just as he had done on the baseball field. Diz had no illusions about his speech. "I'm just a-gonna speak plain, ordinary, workaday English," he said. He resisted all attempts at improving his grammar or his accent.

The fans loved it, though the language purists and many school teachers around St. Louis deplored his butchering of English. A few samples of Dizzy's broadcasting:

"That weren't no balk, dern it! If it'd been a balk, that ol' empire out there at sekint woulda seen it an' a-called it. He ain't gonna let nobody git away with nothin', an' don't you fergit it!"

Another time, as a man slid into a base, he yelled, "Wow! He slud into third and was throwed out!"

Finally a group of citizens got up a petition against him, demanding that he be fired because he was having a bad influence on children. In the midst of all the clamoring after his scalp, Diz calmly said, "A lot o' people who don't say 'ain't' ain't eatin'."

During the war years, it was forbidden for sportscasters to mention weather conditions, lest enemy spies gain valuable information useful in planning bomber attacks. But one afternoon, while Diz was broadcasting, the Cincinnati–St. Louis game was held up by rain.

"Before we go off the air," said Diz, "I cain't tell you folks why this here game has been stopped by the empires, but if y'all will be kind enough to stick your heads out'n your windows, you kin see fer yourselves. And you better hold an umbrella over yer heads when you do."

The aforementioned Frankie Frisch and umpire Bill Klem carried on a colorful feud for years. Their squabbles became baseball classics.

Once, when Klem called out a St. Louis player on a close play at first base, Frisch raced out of the dugout and charged down the base line. But suddenly he stopped and seemed to collapse. Players rushed from both dugouts. It looked as though he had suffered a stroke or a heart attack. As Frankie lay there along the base line and worried players waited for the doctor, Klem strode over in all his blue-suited majesty and elbowed his way through the crowd.

Then, standing over the fallen manager, he pointed his finger and boomed:

"Frisch, dead or alive—you're out of the game."

Another time, frustrated at decisions against the Cardinals by Klem, Frisch brazenly thumbed his nose at the umpire. Klem stormed over to him. "Frisch, did you thumb your nose at me?" he barked.

Sneered Frankie, "You're so good at making decisions —make this one!"

Klem did—and Frankie was out of another game .

When Frisch left the Cardinals to manage at Pittsburgh, the feud continued. One day Danny MacFayden was throwing for the Pirates, and it seemed to the bespectacled pitcher that Klem was calling all the close ones against him. Finally, after another "Ball four!" from Klem, Danny ran off the mound, ripped off his glasses and yelled at Klem, "Here! You need 'em more than I do!"

Klem immediately threw the pitcher out of the game. Out to the plate came Frisch. He tried to calm down the umpire this time, needing his pitcher on the mound. "Have a heart, Bill," he said to Klem. "The kid didn't mean it. He was just excited, that's all."

Klem glared at him. "It was bad enough he was casting aspersions on my eyesight. But he was yelling so loud the stands could hear. He was causing a commotion—inciting a riot. I won't tolerate it!"

Seeing that his plea was useless, Frisch reverted to form. "Well, Bill," he said, "maybe the kid was yelling in case your hearing was as bad as your eyes."

Another of Frisch's targets in blue was umpire Larry Goetz. Once, arguing over a decision, Frisch said, "I'd bet a hundred dollars that man was safe."

"I'd bet a thousand he was out, like I said!" snarled Goetz.

"I'd bet a million he was safe!" shot back Frisch.

"Five million he was out!"

At which point Pirates' catcher, Al Lopez, interrupted. "Could either of you two millionaires lend me ten bucks till payday?" he asked, breaking up the argument.

But it was Klem who stood out above all the umpires as a character. Although at one time he held the position of Chief of Umpires, he never lost the ability to see the humorous side of a situation. The one thing that did get his goat, however, was his nickname, "Catfish." The origins were never known, except that it was probably Art Fletcher, onetime manager of the Phillies, who hung it on him.

Once Ty Cobb came to the plate and started sniffing the air. Klem, incensed at the obvious allusion to his hated nickname, warned Cobb that if he ever did it again he'd have him suspended for a week.

Usually, though, good humor prevailed. One time Klem was being needled by the entire Pittsburgh team. Led by Honus Wagner, the Pirates were really giving the umpire a hard time.

Finally, exasperated, Klem tore off his mask and strode toward the dugout. By the time he got there, however, silence had fallen, broken only by the pretended snores and whistles from the supposedly sleeping players.

Hands on hips, Klem glared at them for a moment, then barked: "All right! If any of you guys wake up before the game is over, I'll run you right out of the park!"

Klem loved to get back at rookies who thought they were smart alecks. Ripper Collins, when he first came up to the Gas House Gang, often gave Klem a bad time.

Klem waited. One day Collins was particularly salty, having struck out three straight times.

The fourth time, Collins hit a drive off the wall down the right-field foul line. He charged around the bases, head down. As he reached second, he heard a voice encouraging him. "Atta boy, all the way, you can make it!"

Ripper turned on the speed. He turned third and heard the voice again "Come on!"

Rip ran down the line and slid into the plate in a cloud of dust. Suddenly Collins realized that the catcher had been standing there, without the ball, and that it had been Klem's voice calling to him.

"Hey, Bill," said Collins, puzzled. "How come you were coaching me?"

"Don't let it bother you," said Klem. "The ball was foul."

The player-manager-umpire feuds still go on, of course, but today's comic operas don't compare with the theatrics of yesteryear. Still, there are some good scenes on stage.

Ron Swoboda came barreling into third base one day, and was called out by umpire Tom Gorman.

"I'm not out!" said Ron.

"Now look here, Ron," said Gorman. "I feel real good today. Went to Mass, and this is a fine Sunday afternoon. So don't spoil it."

"But I'm not out!" insisted Swoboda.

"And why not, pray tell?" said Gorman.

"Because I got the ball," said Swoboda.

"In that case," said Gorman, claiming the umpire's right to the last word, "you're out for interference."

Now that the Mets own a World's Championship, they are weighed down by the responsibility. But in their early days they bore a marvelous resemblance to the Daffy Dodgers of old, and Swoboda had a big part in giving them that image.

Everything about Swoboda marked him as a true Met of the old school. His big hulk, his birthplace (Sparrows Point, Maryland)—even his name. Swoboda is Polish for "freedom." And to add a final fillip, Ron owned a Chinese step-grandfather who sent him Valentines in spring training. A born character, was Swoboda.

As a 20-year-old rookie, he immediately caught the imagination of fans everywhere. In Chicago, kids in the bleachers hung out a banner reading, "Ron Swoboda is really Clark Kent." His home runs and his strikeouts were equal feats of strength, awesome to behold.

The Mets loved Ron to hit homers for more than just the obvious reasons. Hitting homers kept him off the bases. Base running was not one of Ron's specialties. He was terrific at being picked off, and at turning doubles into singles.

Once he hit a tremendous drive off the center-field

fence. But, as he approached second base, he suddenly realized he'd forgotten to touch first—so went back and settled for a single.

"He hits the ball 496 feet, and there he is on first," said manager Casey Stengel after the game. "I guess he's read so much about them 500-foot drives they write about in the papers, and he's never seen one, so he stopped to take a look."

Ron's fielding was also picturesque, if nothing else.

Said Stengel. "He's a little weak on balls in the air. He leaps after them when they ain't there."

Stengel needed all his characteristic good humor to cope with Ron. In the late innings, unless the game was still close, he would take him out of the game, saying, "What if I leave him out there and he runs into a fence? Who's gonna pay for the fence?"

Ron knew his limitations, and took every Met defeat to heart—which meant he had a lot of heartache in those days. Once, after a series of losses, Ron went into a barber shop and slumped wearily into a chair.

"How you want it cut today, Ron?" asked the barber.

"In complete silence, please," answered Swoboda.

The Mets were a haven for misfits and characters still in their formative years. Manager Stengel, the perfect choice to manage such a strange cast of oddballs, had his hands full. After Swoboda, he was presented with Dick

41

Stuart. In a career spanning 13 years, Stuart had gone through 11 cities and eight leagues. Wherever he went, he became a controversial figure. When he arrived at the Mets' spring training camp in 1966, he was known variously as the Man in the Iron Glove, Dr. Strangeglove and "that bum on first."

Stuart developed a thick skin about his reputation as a fielder. He needed it. For eight seasons he either led the league or tied for the lead in errors by a first baseman.

When he was with the Red Sox, the Boston crowd rode him good-naturedly. Once, the Twins Tony Oliva swung at a pitch and the bat flew from his hands, landing at Stuart's feet. When Dick picked it up, the crowd applauded noisily.

After the game, he was asked what he thought about the crowd's reaction.

"That's nothing," Stuart said. "One day in Pittsburgh I caught a hot dog wrapper that was flying around and they gave me a standing ovation."

Stuart moved on, and one day Duke Snider ran into him before an Angels-Padres exhibition game. "I'd have been great in the days of Tinkers-to-Evers-to-Chance," Stuart said to Snider.

"Why?" asked the Duke.

"Because then," chuckled Stuart, "they could have called it Tinkers-to-Evers-to–No Chance."

Take Two and Hit to Right

Fortunately, the Mets retain a bit of their old image. Said relief pitcher Ron Taylor, when he heard he might be traded, "I hope I go to the Yankees. It took me four years to get a rent-controlled apartment in New York."

At Anaheim Stadium, they flash the batter's average on the scoreboard. This prompted 200-pound Tom Egan to remark, during a slump that plummeted him to .117, "I'd rather they posted my weight."

After the new Montreal Expos lost their 20th straight game in 1969, a man of the cloth visited them in the clubhouse at Dodger Stadium. He went to the office of manager Gene Mauch.

"I was talking to some of your Latin boys," he said, "and they asked me to offer a blessing in Spanish. But I can't, I'm only a brother, but I will say a prayer for you in the morning."

"At least we have these people on our side," said Mauch to a reporter. "And it shows you the team may be down, but it hasn't quit."

"How's that?" the reporter asked.

Said Mauch, "The players asked for a blessing—not last rites."

Pitcher Mike Kilkenny, talking about his high school career: "I spent so many years in high school they made four additions to the building and had three different principals while I was there. You know what they put after my picture in the 11th-grade yearbook? It was, 'He'll get a gold watch for long service.' "

National League President Chub Feeney asked Stan Musial what would happen if he took a swing at one of the new lively yellow-stitched balls used in spring training.

Replied Musial: "You'd wonder where the yellow went."

The abundance of Spanish-speaking players in the majors today is taken for granted. But some years ago Cuban pitcher Camilo Pascual, playing for the Twins, was awakened early one morning by a telephone caller, who asked, "Do you speak English?"

"Not at seven in the morning," Pascual said, hanging up.

And recently, Stan Wasiak, Daytona Beach Dodgers' manager, was asked if he had any difficulties in communicating with his Spanish-speaking players.

"No," he replied. "At least, nothing like the players are going to have when I start speaking Polish."

The World Series gets everyone wound up with excitement. Even the umpires feel the tension. The late Larry

Goetz was umpiring one game of the historic Dodger-Yankee Series, the one in which Cookie Lavagetto ruined Floyd Bevens' no-hitter and won for the Dodgers in the ninth inning.

While the Dodgers danced around for joy and hugged each other, Goetz calmly walked around and dusted off the home plate.

The only thing was, the next batter wasn't due until one o'clock the next afternoon.

Richie Allen changed quite a bit when he moved over to the Dodgers. In one of his early games for them, he threw out two runners at the plate from left field. After the game, he said, smiling, "I never even used to throw anybody out from the infield."

Tom Haller is a true hustler. He'll do anything to help the team. He's also determined to make sure everybody else does the same. Once, when Pete Mikkelsen shook off a couple of signs and then was belted, Haller ambled out to the mound and told him, "Listen, I'm out here every day. You come out maybe once, twice a week for a couple innings. *I'll* call the pitches!"

During Willie Stargell's record-breaking homer streak (11 in the month of April, 1971) enemy pitchers were trying to keep the ball away from him. After he'd hit the Mets' Jerry Koosman for his sixth of the month, Koosman came back to the bench and solemnly declared, "No more good ones for him. I'd rather throw him four balls for one base than one ball for four bases."

Slugger Al Kaline was talking to golf pro Ralph Beard about the comparative difficulties of their respective games. Kaline claimed that golfers had it easy. "Look," he said, "you use a club with a flat hitting surface and hit a stationary object. "What's so tough about that? I got to stand up there with a round bat and hit a ball coming at me at maybe 100 miles an hour, and curving."

Replied Beard, "Yeah, but you don't have to go up in the stands and play all your foul balls the way I do!"

George Foster, in his rookie season with the Giants, was talking about Willie Mays—whose shoes he was asked to fill now and again in center field. Said Foster, "Willie's a great guy. He treats me like an equal. The only difference between us is that after the game he heads for the bank and I go to the finance company."

Baseball players have a reputation for being food fanatics. Of course, some can take it or leave it, while others have to be watched by the trainers lest they eat themselves right out of baseball. One spring, when an overweight Billy Loes was having trouble with his control, he was told, "Billy, if you stayed farther away from the table you'd be able to get closer to the plate."

Ballplayers who get food packages from home always have friends around their lockers—friends who are hard to get rid of when the player opens his packages of goodies.

When Ruben Amaro was with the Phillies, he was plagued by these moochers around his locker. His family owned a gourmet delicatessen, and was constantly sending him exotic bits to eat. The worst moocher of all was Amaro's roomie at the time, Ted Savage. Amaro couldn't open a box of anything without Savage suddenly appearing for his share.

One day, Amaro received a package containing such gourmet delights as chocolate-covered ants, grasshoppers and caterpillars. As usual, as soon as he opened the package, Savage came nosying around. "What you got there?" he asked.

Amaro smiled to himself. "Expensive stuff," he said. "From France. So don't take too many."

Savage began digging in. He swallowed a couple of small, chocolate-covered ants, then picked up a large item, wrapped in green foil—a chocolate-covered caterpillar.

"Hey, that's a big one," said Amaro. "Why don't you bite off half and give me the other half?"

"Sure," said Savage, and took a bite. Then he looked at the inside of the chocolate, and his eyes got bigger and bigger. "Say, what is this?" he said.

"That's one of the real good ones," said Amaro. "A caterpillar."

Savage gagged and ran into the bathroom. After gargling and washing out his mouth, he came back to the room, his face white. Amaro held up a jar with other chocolates in it. "Hey, you want some of these?" he asked.

Savage ran out of the room. And nobody ever dug into Amaro's packages again.

When Matta Galante came up for a tryout with the Yankees, the 5-foot 5½-inch second baseman was an obvious target for jibes. Vic Ziegel, the *New York Post* columnist, said, "Galante is the only ballplayer who has to step *up* to get down into the dugout. He's the only ballplayer who sees ground balls go over his head."

And commented broadcaster Joe Garagiola, "Galante has a strike zone from the top of his belt to the bottom of his belt."

Some of the Dodgers were talking about pitchers who like to use the brush-back pitch, and Willie Davis mentioned ex-teammate Don Drysdale. "Don didn't like to see a hitter crowding the plate," he recalled. "Of course, he took the position that you were crowding the plate the moment you left the hitters' circle."

When Leo Durocher took over as manager of the Cubs in 1966, he called the players together and told them he was tired of their conservative playing. "We're going to play the way I like to play," he told them. "We're going to gamble. We're going to run. And I mean *everybody's* going to run."

On opening day, Ron Santo singled. Then, looking over at the third-base coach, he spotted the "steal" sign. A notoriously slow runner, Santo couldn't believe it. The pitch came down, and Santo didn't go. The steal sign remained on, and again Santo didn't go. And a third pitch went by. Santo didn't budge.

At that Durocher got on the top step of the dugout and yelled, loud enough for half the ballpark to hear, "You're goin'!"

Santo got so nervous that he was picked off a moment later.

In the clubhouse after the game, he said, "From now on I'm even out to steal home."

Durocher is practically a legend in his own time. What a career he has had! A player with the old Yankees of Ruth and Gehrig fame, a member of the Gas House Gang, then a career with the Dodgers of Brooklyn, manager of the Giants, then back to the Dodgers of Los Angeles as a coach and finally with the Cubs as a manager again.

During the course of his long, stormy, colorful career, Leo earned his nickname "The Lip" for his running battle with the umpires. Leo was one of the best.

He was coaching at third for the LA Dodgers during a game in Chicago when umpire Frank Dascoli called the game on account of darkness. The Dodgers, trailing, were stuck with a loss. Incensed, Durocher ran over to Dascoli and asked why he was calling the game so suddenly.

"Because I can't see, that's why," replied the umpire.

"So what!" cracked Leo, "you haven't seen all day either!"

A good friend of Leo's is Danny Kaye, the comedian. Danny, a hot Dodger fan, regularly occupies a third-base box. Naturally, when Durocher was with the Dodgers in the coaching box, Kaye would loudly defend him against the umpires.

One day, when Leo was engaged in an inning-by-inning battle with Augie Donatelli, Kaye joined in from his box. Finally, Augie had enough of it. He went to Leo.

"Durocher," he said, "get that guy off my back or you're out of the game."

Leo went over to Kaye's box. "Danny," he said. "Do me a favor. Don't do me any favors!"

Take Two and Hit to Right

Back in the days before night baseball, when Leo was still playing a pretty good shortstop for the Brooklyn Dodgers, the second half of a Giants-Dodgers doubleheader began rather late one afternoon. Dusk was already falling, and on the mound for the Giants was a wild-armed hurler named Roy Parmelee.

Up to the plate came Leo. Parmelee whipped over two strikes, then threw a "waste" pitch under Leo's chin. Durocher threw his bat down and walked to the dugout.

"Hey, wait a minute!" yelled the plate umpire. "That was a ball!"

Leo shook his head. "That was strike three and I'm out," he said. "I'm not standing up there anymore!"

When Hank Aaron hit his 600th homer to become only the third player in history to reach that mark (Babe Ruth and Willie Mays are the other two), they trotted out the story of Hank's early days in the majors. He was so quiet that he looked almost asleep at the plate. Once Roy Campanella tried to needle him, saying, "Hey Hank, you're holding your bat wrong. Don't you know you're supposed to hold it so you can read the label?"

"Didn't come up here to read," replied Aaron.

The baseball writers were talking about third basemen, comparing their abilities to play the bunt. Names like Red Rolfe and Spider Jorgensen and, of course, Pie Traynor were mentioned, and someone named Oakland's Sal Bando as a good one. Then one of the writers nominated George Kell as one of the fastest, relating this tale of Kell's rookie season with old Athletics of Philadelphia.

The veteran Bobo Newsom was on the mound that afternoon for the A's. Newsom, who'd lost the zip off his fast one by then, was getting along on junk pitches. The game was close when the Tigers got a man on first in the eighth inning. The next batter stepped up, obviously with the intention of trying to bunt the runner along.

Every time Bobo came down with the pitch, Kell charged down from third to field the bunt. Meanwhile, Bobo was giving it all he could. Finally, with the count three-and-one. Newsom called Kell over for a chat.

"What are you trying to do to me?" he demanded of the rookie third baseman.

"What do you mean?" asked the puzzled Kell. "I'm supposed to be breaking down the line with the pitch, ain't I?"

"Yeah," growled Bobo, "but do you have to do it so fast? You're gettin' down to the plate quicker than the ball!"

Pitchers are the absolute masters at finding outrageous excuses for poor performances or playing lapses. Billy Loes is responsible for an immortal moment in Dodger history with this incident during the 1952 World Series.

Loes was pitching for the Dodgers against the Yankees,

and holding them scoreless. Meanwhile, the Dodgers opened a slim lead. Then, in the sixth inning, the Yankees started a rally and got men on base with two out. Bearing down, Loes got the next batter to tap to the mound. Billy went for it, bobbled it, kicked it, then couldn't find it at all. The runner was safe.

Now, completely rattled by his own error, Loes blew up. The Yankees knocked him out of the box and went on to win the game.

Later, in the clubhouse, the unhappy young pitcher put himself among the immortals with a great line. When a sports writer said to him, "What happened on that ground ball, Billy?" Loes replied, stammering, "I—I lost it in the sun."

It took a Dodger to say that one, as it took a Dodger to put a new wrinkle on it a few years later. It was now the era of night baseball, and Sandy Koufax was pitching against the Mets. Of course, Koufax needed no funny lines to get himself into the books; his pitching arm proclaimed his immortality. Still, Sandy had a dry sense of humor to go with his fantastic pitching talent.

This night against the Mets, he was nursing a 2–0 lead when the Mets rallied and got men on first and second with nobody out. The next batter, attempting to bunt the runners around, looped the ball to the mound instead. Sandy reached for it, but the ball glanced off his glove, and everybody was safe.

Sandy got out of trouble in his usual style, striking out the next batter and getting Ed Kranepool to bounce into a double play.

When he returned to the dugout, Sandy was greeted by Don Drysdale, who said to him, "Hey, Sandy, how'd you miss that easy looper?"

Koufax shrugged. "I lost it in the moon."

Sam McDowell was keeping them low on the hitters one night in Cleveland, and umpire Hank Soar was calling most of them balls. Everytime Soar would call one of the low ones a ball, Sam would shake his head in disbelief. Finally, McDowell himself came to bat. Tiger hurler Joe Coleman came in with the first pitch—at the knees. Soar's right hand went up.

"Whatta you mean, strike?" asked McDowell. "A pitch down there is a ball!"

The plate umpire smiled sweetly. "That's what I've been trying to tell you for the past three innings!"

Denny McLain, brash young rookie that he was, thought he had to give excuses for bad pitches. Once, after Harmon Killebrew had socked him for a homer, he came back to the dugout and said, "That pitch got away, but he won't be hitting any more homers off me!"

"Why not?" said Mayo Smith, then the Tigers' skipper. "You planning on leaving baseball?"

The fabulous Lefty Grove was a sore loser, too, continually grumbling about hard luck that caused him to lose close ball games. One day, shortly after dropping a couple of close ones, he took the mound in the first inning, turned around and glared at the infield.

"It's ol' Lefty pitching today," he said loudly, "and you know what's gonna happen? I'm probably gonna lose 1–0 because one of you guys is gonna make an error in the eighth or ninth inning!"

Then there was Harry Taylor of the Dodgers. He started one World Series game against the Yankees by walking the first three men to face him. Out to the mound rushed Clyde Sukeforth, the Dodger coach.

"What's the matter?" asked Sukey.

"Why, nothing," said Taylor. "Nothing at all. I'm just fine."

Sukeforth took a look around the infield. "Then what's all them guys doing on the bases?" he asked.

"Oh," said Taylor, "I'm just pacing myself."

"Is that so?" barked Sukey. "Well you can just get into the clubhouse and pace the floor while we get somebody in here to pitch!"

Lefty Gomez was having his troubles, in the twilight of a great career with the Yankees, and, one afternoon, he was being rocked pretty hard by the White Sox.

"Lefty, you gotta throw harder," said coach Art Fletcher on the bench.

"Art," sighed Lefty, "I'm throwin' twice as hard as I ever have—only the ball just ain't goin' so fast!"

Things happened to Lefty even after he left the Yankees and went to the minor leagues as manager of their Binghamton club. One day his boys, trailing by a run in the ninth inning, rallied to put men on first and second with nobody out.

The pitcher came up, and naturally Lefty called for the bunt. The pitcher stuck his bat out at the first pitch and cracked it sharply to the mound. The enemy pitcher whirled and threw to third. One out. The third baseman whipped the ball to second. Two out. Then the shortstop threw to first for a triple play.

All the while, the batter just stood at home plate watching the ball being whipped around the infield.

In the third-base coaching box, Gomez dropped to his knees and lifted his face heavenward.

"What's with you?" barked the umpire.

"I'm asking forgiveness," moaned Gomez. "It was all my fault, all my fault!"

"If you ask me, it was your dumb hitter's fault," said the umpire.

"No, no," protested Gomez. "I told him to bunt, and he tried. I'm the only one to blame."

"But if he'd run he'd have beaten it out, Lefty," said the umpire.

"That's just it," replied Gomez. "I only told him to bunt. I forgot to tell him to run!"

Another time, Binghamton had a 1–0 lead in the ninth, but the other side got a man to second base with one out. A rookie pitcher was on the mound. The kid was stalling, kicking the dirt and looking around. Gomez figured the pressure was getting to the youngster, so he rushed over and tried to calm him down, calling for time.

As he stood at the mound talking, Gerry Coleman came running over from his second-base position. "Aw, what'd you have to go and spoil it for, Lefty?" he said. "We had it all set up for the hidden-ball trick!"

The knuckleball has practically disappeared from baseball. Modern pitchers stick to the fast ball, the slider and the change-up. They don't even trust curves, much less the old knuckler. And with good reason. It has an unreliable history.

One of the great knuckleball artists of all time was Fat Freddie Fitzsimmons, who knocked around the National League quite a bit. Nobody liked to hit against Fitz's knuckler. One day, the Redbirds' Rip Collins was at the plate. Spotting the knuckler coming at him, Rip practically closed his eyes and swung. The ball dropped into right center for a base hit.

As Collins took his turn around first, Fitzsimmons bawled at him, "Ripper, you had no business hittin' that pitch. How could you know where it was goin' when I didn't know where it was goin' myself?"

Hoyt Wilhelm has spent so many years in baseball that his experiences cover a couple of generations of players. Hoyt is one of those clever pitchers whose ability to get by with "junk" kept him going when everyone else his age had long since departed. One day, when he was tantalizing the Dodgers with his slow stuff, he hit Duke Snider on the head. Duke stood there, stunned for a moment, and then allowed himself to be led away to the clubhouse.

Later, when Wilhelm had a chance to stop by and see him, he said to Snider, "Fine pal you are. You could at least have fallen down and made my stuff look good!"

Earl Stephenson, the Cubs' young bullpen star, managed to do a little pitching while on duty as a paratrooper. He was hurling for his camp against another Army troop one day, and getting belted pretty regularly.

At one point, three men in a row hit whistling line drives through the infield for base hits. The second baseman called time and trotted over. "Hey, Earl, bear down," the man said. "You trying to get us killed out there?"

"What are *you* worrying about?" replied Stephenson. "Who's nearer those bats, you or me?"

Lots of pitchers have been accused of throwing the illegal "spitter"—especially when they're big winners. One steaming August day, Denny McLain was wiping the perspiration from his forehead when the batter, Tony Conigliaro, yelled at him, "Hey, that ain't legal, McLain!"

"What ain't legal?" replied Denny. "Sweatin'?"

But, telling funny stories about pitchers, one inevitably gets back to Lefty "Goofy" Gomez. He kept the Yankees winning and laughing for many years. Lefty was ready to talk and argue about anything, with anybody. Once he and Babe Ruth got into a hot discussion about how to pitch when there were two men on base. Though the mighty Babe was by then famous as a slugger, he had started his career as a pitcher—and a good one, at that.

The argument, which took place in a hotel lobby while the Yankees were on a road trip, waxed hot and heavy, and it was after midnight by the time the two of them agreed they couldn't agree.

"You know what?" said Lefty finally. "Let's go see Joe McCarthy. Maybe he can settle it for us."

Gomez and Ruth promptly rushed to manager McCarthy's room. Lefty rapped on the door.

"What is it?" demanded a sleepy voice from inside.

"It's me and the Babe," called Gomez. "We want you to settle an important question for us."

"At one o'clock in the morning!" yelled McCarthy. "Go away and let me sleep! See me tomorrow!"

"What? Do you want us to leave those poor guys on base all night?" demanded Gomez indignantly.

Another classic Gomez rejoinder was recorded after a season when he could only win 11 while losing 15. His $25,000 salary was threatened with a cut to $7,500 by owner Jake Ruppert. "Tell you what, Colonel," Gomez said. "You can keep the salary and give me the cut."

One dark and gloomy afternoon, the Yankees were facing Bob Feller, the famous Cleveland fireballer. As the afternoon wore on and it got darker and gloomier, the Yankee hitters were becoming ever more nervous about standing in against the sometimes wild bullet serves of Rapid Robert.

The Yankees fell behind, and in the late innings McCarthy pinch-hit for the pitcher. In came Gomez, in relief.

When it came Lefty's turn to bat, it was really dark. Bravely he took his place, standing as far away from the plate as is legally possible.

Then, just as Feller started his big windup, Lefty took

a kitchen match from his hip pocket and lit it on the thick end of the bat.

"Hey!" squawked the plate umpire. "Whatta you think you're doing, Gomez? Can't you see Feller's getting ready to pitch?"

"I can see *him* all right," replied Lefty, "but I want to make darn sure he can see *me!*"

Another time Gomez was facing Jimmy Foxx, the great Athletics slugger. Catcher Bill Dickey hung out one sign after the other, but Lefty kept shaking him off.

Finally, Dickey went out to the mound. "Look, Lefty," he said, "you're going to have to throw something. Why don't you pitch?"

"Let's wait a while," Gomez said. "Maybe he'll get a long-distance phone call."

Lefty broke into baseball with the Salt Lake club in the old Utah-Idaho League. Even then he loved a good laugh almost as much as a good win. Once, he got into a discussion with a young umpire before a game, and both men talked about their ambitions to make it to the major leagues.

Then the game began. Lefty went to the mound, and the umpire took his place behind the plate.

Lefty threw, and the umpire called, "Ball one!"

Lefty threw again, and again the umpire called the

pitch a ball. Twice more Lefty threw, twice more the umpire called a ball and the batter trotted off to first.

Lefty came halfway down off the mound and called out to the umpire, "You keep calling 'em that way, brother, and *neither* of us is going to the big leagues!"

That jump to the big leagues scares many a rookie. The gulf between the minors and the majors is a vast one. Even such Hall of Fame greats as Ted Williams found that the Big Jump brought Big Problems.

Shortly after he joined the Red Sox, the great left-handed hitter went into a terrible batting slump. He became deeply depressed and unhappy. To a reporter who happened to catch him deep in the dumps one day, Ted confided that he wished he could have been a fireman instead of a baseball player, and thus have avoided all the problems that were plaguing him at the moment.

This was a good story, and naturally the reporter told it around the ball park.

The next day, Boston faced the White Sox in Chicago. When Ted came to bat for the first time, a roar went up from the crowd. The clowns in the White Sox lineup had appeared in front of their dugout dressed in fire hats, dragging a hose and making sounds like fire sirens.

Suddenly the roar of laughter in the stadium changed to gasps of surprise. Just outside the ball park a lumber yard began to go up in flames. As thick black smoke and yellow tongues of flame shot skyward, fire engines clanged madly past the stadium, their sirens screaming full blast.

At the plate, meanwhile, Ted Williams, a rookie with a sense of humor, was holding his sides with laughter.

"Boy, when they pull a gag on you in the majors," he gasped between giggles, "they sure give it all they got!"

When the inimitable Dick Stuart broke in with the Pirates, he had the misfortune to face Sandy Koufax one night early in his rookie debut. Under the lights Sandy was always bewildering, but this night he was impossible. Nobody could touch him. As the innings wore on, he got tougher and tougher, faster and faster.

Stuart didn't even get close to him the first two times up; he waved futilely at the night air.

Now it was his third time at bat. Sandy wound up and blazed the ball over. Stuart stood there gaping, the bat never leaving his shoulder. When the third blazer popped into the catcher's mitt and the umpire called strike three, Stuart turned around and said, "Hey ump, don't you think that last one sounded a little low?"

Another wacky Pittsburgher of the day was Rocky Nelson. One afternoon, soon after joining the club from the minors, Rocky socked a triple. The club was six runs behind at the time, but, all excited about his big hit and anxious to show his stuff, Rocky tried to steal home on the first pitch and was thrown out by six feet.

When he got back to the dugout, Billy Meyer screamed

at him, "What did you pull a bonehead stunt like that for?"

Nelson shrugged. "Now you know why they call me Rocky."

Few rookies ever reported to a major-league training camp with the credentials of Bobby Brown. When he came up to the Yankees, he had already completed his medical internship and was duly called "Doc" by his new team-mates.

Casey Stengel seemed to be the most enthusiastic of all. "Boy, am I glad to see you!" he gushed when Bobby reported on the field.

Brown was dumbfounded. The Yankees had a good third baseman in Billy Johnson, and another highly touted rookie infielder named Gil McDougald. So what was the big deal?

"Yeah," continued Stengel. "I couldn't wait till you got here, Brown. Tell me, what have you got for these bunions on my toes?"

Casey Stengel is a book in himself, regardless of his *serious* contributions to baseball. Casey was endowed with a tremendous sense of the ridiculous in life, a sense of humor that came to his rescue whenever the alternative to laughter would have been to club himself to death with a baseball bat or drown himself in the water bucket.

Take Two and Hit to Right

Casey spent many years managing the old Brooklyn Dodgers, a job that could give an ulcer ulcers. The Dodgers drew more laughs than fans in those days. The first division was something they only read about in the sports pages. Among the oddball assortment of baseball misfits Casey looked after was a pitcher aptly named Boom-Boom Beck. The nickname was the result of the sound usually heard in the ball park when Beck was pitching.

One day poor Boom-Boom was being belted even harder than usual, and the baseballs were booming off the walls like supersonic jets breaking the sound barrier. Finally Casey wearily waved him off the mound.

Angrily, Beck threw the ball on a line against the concrete wall and stormed into the dugout. Stengel sat there patiently.

"Now that last one looked like a pretty good pitch to me," said Casey, "probably the best one you threw all day. Would you like us to build a concrete wall for you behind the plate so's you'll have a better target?" Stengel let the barb sink in a moment, then continued, "Or do you think it would be a better idea to put the concrete wall in front of the plate someplace? Say, between you and the hitter?"

Beck, fuming, got up and walked to the end of the bench, kicking at the water bucket.

"Hey, cut that out," called Casey. "If you break your toes, I won't be able to trade you!"

Once Casey was persuaded to bring a highly touted kid outfielder up from Little Rock. In the rookie's first game he muffed two easy fly balls in the early innings, each time complaining about the wind in Ebbets Field.

Then, in the ninth, the kid dropped another one, letting the winning runs score.

In the clubhouse later he was still making excuses. "It was that wind out there, that darned wind!" he said to Stengel.

"That was them trade winds, son," Casey declared. "You're going back to Little Rock!"

Another of Casey's charges was Frenchy Bordagary. The little second baseman, the only man then in baseball to sport a mustache, gave Casey many moments of anguish. Frenchy had his own way of doing things wrong, and an alibi to go with every bonehead play.

One day, in a game against the Giants, Frenchy fanned three straight times. Each time he had an excuse—the umpire was blind; the pitcher was using a spitter; the bat slipped.

His fourth time at bat, Frenchy managed to tap one out in front of the plate. Catcher Gus Mancuso pounced on the ball and threw out Frenchy easily.

When Bordagary returned to the dugout ready to unload his latest alibi, Casey was prepared for him.

"I know, I know," Stengel said, in mock sympathy, "the catcher was playing too far in on that one."

Ol' Case wasn't too hard on his boys, though, no doubt because he himself had been a bit of a character as an active player. Casey gave tough John McGraw many a restless night. Stengel's roommate on the Giants then was Bob "Irish" Meusel, and the two of them lived it up pretty well at night. Finally, manager McGraw hired a private detective to shadow both of them.

When Stengel found out about it, he stormed into Mc-Graw's office. "I'm as good an outfielder as Meusel is," he shouted, "and I deserve a private detective all to myself!"

"No, you're not as good as Meusel," replied McGraw. "And I can't afford to hire two private detectives anyway. So you're gonna have to go, Stengel!"

Shortly afterward, Casey found himself shipped to the Boston Braves.

Some 12 years later, Casey returned to Boston as manager. Things weren't much better there than at Brooklyn, from whence he'd come.

Casey had a pitcher named Al Javery, nicknamed "Beartracks." Al didn't do all that badly for a pitcher toiling for a seventh-place club. But during his rookie season, when he finished 2–4, he had some awful moments.

Casey started him against the Pirates one day, with Phil Masi catching.

The first batter of the ball game whacked the first ball off the center-field fence for a triple. The next one homered on the first pitch. Javery hit the third batter with his first pitch, and the next one doubled, again on the first pitch.

Casey walked slowly out to the mound, and Masi came out to join him near the hill.

"What's the story?" said the manager to his catcher. "Ain't he got his stuff?"

"I dunno," said Masi. "I ain't caught it yet."

One spring, desperate for some hitting, Casey watched with interest as a big rookie slammed the ball off the fences and out of the park. After the batting session, Stengel walked over to the youngster. "What position do you play, kid?" he asked.

"Anything," replied the eager rookie. "First, the outfield. Even catch if you want."

Casey took him at his word and tried him at a number of positions. At all of them he was found wanting. Sadly, Casey retired him to the bench as a pinch hitter.

"What's the idea?" the rookie complained. "You can't put a .400 hitter like me on the bench!"

"The trouble is," said Casey, "you're also a .400 fielder. So sit down!"

A similar story is told about the young outfielder trying to impress Stengel with his glove work one day. On a fly ball to center field, the kid, playing in right, dashed all the way over and tried to make a circus catch, when the center fielder could have caught it in his hip pocket. Naturally, the kid messed up the play, and the ball bounced off his glove for a double.

In the dugout after the inning, Casey gave the rookie a dressing down. The kid defended himself.

"But gee, Skipper, I catch balls like that easy nine times out of ten."

"So what?" snorted Stengel. "Who needs an outfielder who fields only .900?"

Casey's long service and experience were finally rewarded when he got the Yankees to manage in 1949, and he promptly ran off with five straight World's Championships. True enough, he had fabulous material to work with, as some cynics said. But Casey never denied that he had walked into a dream situation. In fact, during spring training that first season, when several reporters inquired about how he was distributing the coaching chores, Casey replied, with his famous wink, "Dickey's gonna coach the catchers, Jim Turner, the pitchers, Crosetti, the infielders, and me—I'll coach DiMaggio."

Casey's own night-owling capers under McGraw helped him understand the curfew-breaking activities of some of his Yankee stars. There was Don Larsen, for example. Shortly after pitching the only perfect game in World Series history, Larsen went to spring training in St. Petersburg, Florida. The town is famous as a haven for retired persons, a peaceful, sleepy community.

At five o'clock one Sunday morning, Larsen managed to wrap his new car around a lamppost and get his name in the papers. Stengel was asked that day if he was going to fine Larsen.

Winked Casey, "Anybody who can find something to do at five o'clock in the morning in St. Petersburg deserves a medal, not a fine."

If Casey had a few problems with the Yankees, they were of a different stripe from the ones he encountered with the Dodgers and Braves—and later would encounter with the Mets.

One of Casey's problem children on his champion Yankee clubs was Yogi Berra—who became almost as famous a "character" as Case himself.

Yogi came up to the Yankees as a free-swinging rookie. Overanxious, he got into the habit of swinging on the first pitch, no matter where it was thrown.

After one such incident, which ended with Berra's striking out, Casey got him aside and said, "Listen, kid, when you're up there with the bat, you gotta think!"

Yogi looked at him, puzzled. "Skip," he said, "how can I think and hit, too?"

Much of Yogi's wit was of the unconscious kind, at least in his early days. That is to say, in his ingenuous way he didn't realize he was being funny.

After Don Larsen pitched that history-making World

Series no-hitter, the Yankee dressing room quite naturally was bedlam. Reporters, TV cameramen and well-wishers crowded the room, yelling themselves hoarse.

Sitting by himself on a stool was Yogi, calmly puffing on a cigarette. As one of the regular sports writers passed by the stool, rushing toward Larsen, Yogi said to him, "Hi, kid, what's new?"

Jimmy Piersall, whose life story was made into a movie ("Fear Strikes Out"), kept up a running battle of words with Yogi. After a siege of mental illness, Jimmy came back to play with the Red Sox. He was batting against the Yankees in a game that was marred by some particularly close brush-back pitching.

When he came to bat late in the game, the two batters previous to Jimmy's appearance had been knocked down by the Yankee pitcher. Piersall dug in and said to Berra, "Look, if this guy throws at me, I'll wrap this bat around your neck—and I'm the one guy who can do it and get away with it. I can plead temporary insanity."

Replied Yogi, "Look, boy, on this club we don't knock down no .250 hitters."

Yogi also became well known for his assaults on the English language. Ill with a stomach ache one day, he said to Stengel, "Case, I can't play today. I got pantomime poisoning."

Another time Joe Page, the Yankees' bullpen ace of

the 1940s, was telling Yogi of a hunting trip he once took with Enos Slaughter, the Cardinals' slugger.

"Slaughter loves to hunt," said Page, "and he dashed in and out of the bushes so much he got a cyst on his back."

Berra laughed and said, "Now what kind of a bird is a cyst?"

Yogi and Phil Rizzuto were great friends, and business associates outside of baseball. When Phil left the Yankees to become a broadcaster, the friendship continued. One morning, driving over to Yankee Stadium together from New Jersey, Berra said, "My wife told me that during yesterday's broadcast you said that I kept talking all through the game. I didn't talk much, did I?"

"Not much you didn't," laughed Rizzuto. "When you reached first base, you began jawing with the first baseman and the umpire. You did the same thing when you got to second base. Again at third. And when you were catching, you never stopped talking to the umpire and the hitters.

"Tell me, Yogi," Rizzuto said. "What were you saying to them?"

Berra shrugged. "I don't remember. I never say anything important anyway."

Considering Stengel's storied career, it was inevitable that he would wind up managing the Mets. Nobody else in baseball could have fit into the Mets' comic-opera baseball style the way Casey did. The early days of the team could perhaps be summarized in the person of Marvelous Marv Throneberry.

Marv played first base with all the cuteness and ferocity of a puppy dog attacking a bedroom slipper. He became a New York folk hero. Somebody wrote, "Marvelous Marv does more than play first for the Mets. He *is* the Mets."

A typical Marvelous Marv boner was pulled one night against the Dodgers, in Shea Stadium. In the ninth inning, Marv hit what appeared to be a game-winning inside-the-park home run. The Mets' fans whooped and shrieked with joy—which turned into howls of chagrin a moment later when the umpire, acting on a protest, called Throneberry out for failing to touch first.

Wearily, Casey stomped out to protest. But on his way he passed Cookie Lavagetto, the first-base coach.

"Casey, don't argue too long with the ump," Cookie whispered. "Marv missed touching second base, too!"

Ed Kranepool remembers those Mets well; he was practically the "old man" of Shea Stadium when they became champs. Ed remembers, too, his own rookie days at first base, and one play in particular when he pulled a "Marvelous Marv" boob.

Young and eager, anxious to make good, Ed dreamed of the situation which would enable him to make the toughest double play of them all—first to second to first.

Then, in a game against the Cardinals at Shea Stadium, with men on first and second, the batter hit a sharp bouncer right to him. Too far off the bag to touch it and then throw to second, he threw to second immediately—and hurled the ball wildly into center field. Everybody was safe. The Cardinals went on to score two runs.

On the bench after the inning was over, Stengel said to him, "Kranepool, the next time you try to start a double play with *two out,* it'll cost you money!"

Veteran baseball observers regard the Phillies of 1930 as close cousins of the early Mets. But then, Philadelphia has always been a strange baseball town. The fact that the Phillies found it necessary to trade away a player like Richie Allen testifies to the unique relationship between the fans and their baseball team in Philadelphia.

Sports writer Red Smith loved to stick his pen into the hide of Philadelphia, probably because he loved baseball so much. When he was writing his column for the now defunct New York *Herald Tribune,* he used to tell of the days at the old Baker Bowl, when the Phillies played there to an audience consisting largely of sports writers and relatives of the players.

To amuse themselves, the writers, sitting in the many-tiered press box, would throw paper clips, popcorn, peanuts and assorted rubbish on the heads of the writers in the bottom row.

One day some Chicago writers were in town, and, bored with the usual missile throwing, they let go paper cups filled with water. Inevitably, the water began trickling through the floorboards down to the grandstand.

This brought Gerry Nugent, then president of the club, upstairs to the press box, quivering with indignation.

"I beg you to remember," he said, "that we have customers downstairs!"

At this Warren Brown of Chicago jumped from his chair as though jabbed with a needle.

"Holy cow!" he cried, "what a story!"

But to get back to the Met-like Phillies of 1930—this was a team that had eight men hitting .313 or better, yet finished last, 40 games behind the pennant winners, the Cardinals.

The captain of the team, second baseman Fresco Thompson, hit a "lowly" .282 that year.

"I could have hit .300, though," Thompson recalled some years later. "I was going along fine, hitting around .320, but the others guys were so ashamed of my average they wouldn't let me take batting practice. I wasn't even allowed to speak to O'Doul and Klein." (Lefty O'Doul hit .383; Chuck Klein hit .386, with 40 homers and 170 runs batted in.)

"Yeah, I was captain," Thompson continued. "But it

was more like being foreman of a chain gang. Who'd pay any attention to a hitter like me?"

How could a team with hitters like that finish last? Unfortunately, they also had to take the field every inning.

Burt Shotton, who managed the club (and came out of retirement many years later to pilot pennant-winning Dodger teams), had one of the worst pitching staffs ever assembled anywhere. Earlier in this chapter, Boom-Boom Beck was mentioned. Well, *every* Philly pitcher could have earned Beck's nickname. (Beck himself came to the Phillies in 1939.) The noise from the ball parks where the Phillies played sounded like artillery fire. While their own hitters were bombarding enemy hurling with an average of 6.8 runs per game and 11.4 hits per game, Philly pitchers set a record by giving up more—7.7 runs per game.

The pitchers got no help from the fielders. The club made 236 errors. With the short Baker Bowl walls, the outfielders found themselves ducking ricochets like flying bullets. Klein set a record of 44 assists by an outfielder that year.

A typical Philadelphia sports page headline of 1930 read: KLEIN HITS 2, HURTS 1, PHILS LOSE.

Let's return to Richie Allen. He was never happy with Philadelphia, and he welcomed his switch to the Dodgers. He had always been friendly with the Dodger players, especially Don Drysdale. This might have been because

Drysdale owns horses, and Richie is crazy about horses. Not owning them—riding. Richie has nursed a secret ambition for years.

"I'd love to be a jockey," he said once. "I'd like to drop 90 pounds in the morning, get out to the racetrack, ride as a jockey and then gain back the weight and come back to the ball park at night at 195."

He said to Drysdale. "When you gonna let me be your jockey?"

Don replied, "When I start raising elephants."

The apathy of Philadelphia baseball fans is not entirely without foundation, of course. There hasn't been much exciting baseball played there since the famous "Whiz Kids" teams of 1950–51.

Other major-league cities have suffered similarly. Which brings up the Joe Garagiola story of the father telling his baseball-fanatic son that if he worked hard he might one day grow up to be President.

"What!" exclaimed the boy, "and have to root for the Senators!"

Garagiola wasn't as bad a hitter as he often makes out in his stories, but he has found life more profitable as an afterdinner speaker and broadcaster than he did as a catcher for the Cardinals and Pirates in the 1950s. The Pirates of 1952, in fact, were molded in the fashion of the old Dodgers, the 1930 Phillies and the Mets of a decade later.

Joe hit .316 in the 1946 World Series, soon after coming back from service in the South Pacific. Whatever else he did out there, he was best remembered by many GIs around Manila for a long clout over the right-field wall of Rizal Stadium. The author well remembers seeing Joe's name inscribed on that wall—next to the name of some Japanese soldier who had apparently slugged one during the occupation of the Philippines.

By the time Joe got to the Pirates, the eminent Branch Rickey was in the process of rebuilding the team with young players. "Operation Peach Fuzz" the plan was called.

One day in Cincinnati, Bubba Church was going for the Reds, and held a two-run lead in the ninth. Then Gus Bell led off for the Pirates with a homer. Ralph Kiner homered, and Joe himself followed with a third straight homer, to break the tie.

Bobby Del Greco, one of the Buc youngsters, went up next. On the first pitch he went down. On the second pitch he went down again. Then, after the count had gone to two and two, he flied to the left fielder. Del Greco returned to the bench and sat down next to Clyde McCullough, a 15-year veteran.

"Man, he's wild," Bobby said. "And I thought he was supposed to have good control."

McCullough took him by the shoulder and said, "Son, when the three previous hitters have belted one out of the park, go up there and go down before you see the whites of his eyes!"

Garagiola always maintained that, if there had to be a new way found to lose games, the Pirates would have found it that year.

One night Augie Donatelli was umpiring at first base in a game against the Brooklyn Dodgers. At first base for the Pirates was George Metkovich. As usual, Buc hurlers were being bombed. Line drives were shrieking past Metkovich like shrapnel.

Finally, Duke Snider hit a grasscutter that bounced off George's shin and skidded into right field for a single.

Metkovich looked at Donatelli and yelled, "For cripes sake, Augie, don't just stand there. Get a glove and help me out!"

Another of the club's problems was that the new kids had trouble learning the signs. Garagiola recalled a game against Brooklyn when Fred Haney was managing the Bucs. With the count on the batter one and one, Haney gave the steal sign to a rookie on first. Catcher Roy Campanella suspected the steal was on, and called for a pitch-out. Nothing happened.

Haney gave the sign again; Campy figured the sign was still on, and again called for the pitch-out. Still the kid on first didn't make a move.

Campanella decided that he had the sign figured wrong, but, though Haney flashed it a third time, the kid remained rooted to the bag.

Haney called time and beckoned to the rookie.

"Did you get that steal sign?" he asked.

"Yeah, I got it."

"Well, I gave it three times. Why didn't you go?"

"I didn't think you meant it," the kid replied.

In later years Garagiola's favorite topic of conversation became Yogi Berra. One day Joe was telling about Yogi's first few weeks on the Norfolk team. Berra had a notoriously erratic arm when he first broke in. According to Garagiola, in Berra's first two weeks at Norfolk, 17 men who tried to steal second were thrown out at third— by an outfielder.

Yogi also had trouble fielding bunts. In fact, before one game the Norfolk manager bet him a steak dinner he couldn't throw a batter out at first base.

During the game, Yogi himself was batting, and he hit a little dribbler out in front of the plate. Before the catcher or the pitcher could move, Yogi jumped out, grabbed the ball and threw it to first base.

Then he went back to the dugout, grinning and demanded his steak dinner.

Joe and Yogi became good personal friends. After one particularly bad day, when Yogi fanned three times,

Garagiola accompanied him out to his home in New Jersey. All during dinner Yogi remained silent, until finally his wife, Carmen, said to him, "Don't take it so badly. Forget the game. It's over. Think about me."

Yogi looked at her balefully. "Three times today I would have traded you for a base hit."

It helps to explain the eccentricities of Yogi Berra when one realizes that he was a catcher. The men in the iron masks are a breed unto themselves—like the pitchers whose serves they receive. Maybe it's the punishment they take—the split thumbs and the broken pinkies and the foul ticks clanking against their masks—but there is no doubt that catchers are often very funny people.

The legends of Larry McLean, for example, have been handed down until this very day. Larry McLean was a hard-working, colorful catcher with the New York Giants. Larry made life miserable for his manager, the fabulous John McGraw, a tough little character himself. It was one of Larry's weaknesses that he liked to relax his aching legs, after a long day of knee-bending behind the plate, by doing a little elbow-bending in the evenings—at the neighborhood bar, that is.

It was the afternoon after one such relaxing evening that the still slightly woozy McLean was working a game behind the plate. With an enemy runner on third base, the shaky catcher let a pitch dribble out of his glove.

Hastily throwing off his mask, Larry pounced on the ball and whirled around in time to see the runner trying to score from third.

Larry blinked, shook his head, got his eyes back in focus and dashed for the plate to cut off the runner. He arrived there at the same time as the umpire, who had closed in to cover the play; the pitcher, who had charged in from the mound to take a possible throw; the runner, who was roaring in like an express train; and the batter, who was standing there fascinated by the whole thing.

Since he was operating in sort of a haze, all that poor, hung-over Larry could see were four blurry figures dancing around home plate. Without stopping to figure it out, Larry quickly slammed the ball on the runner, the pitcher, the umpire and the batter in quick succession.

"I don't know who the runner is," he shouted, "but one of you guys is out!"

Tough little McGraw (Little Napoleon, they called him) had a soft spot for McLean, as he did for most of his men with personality quirks. The fiery manager tried everything to get McLean to stay on the wagon. But poor McLean's love for the bottle finally ruined him as a player, though his end came in a rather odd fashion.

McGraw finally put a tail on Larry to keep him on the straight and narrow. For a while this worked, but then Larry slipped again, and word was brought to McGraw. Larry learned of this, and mistakenly blamed one of McGraw's scouts for turning him in. Furious, Larry fumed for weeks, waiting for a moment to get his revenge, One evening he caught up with the scout in a hotel lobby. The man was sitting with McGraw on a bench surrounding a bubbling fountain. McLean bore down on him, shouting accusations.

"You're crazy, McLean," the scout said, mildly. "I never did no such thing."

"You're a liar!" yelled McLean. "I'll teach you to spy on me!" And with that, the powerful catcher lifted the scout in the air and tossed him into the fountain.

McGraw leaped to his feet, purple with rage. "Look here, Larry," he snapped, "you can't treat my scout like that!"

"I can't, eh!" snorted McLean. "Not only him, but you too!" He picked up little McGraw and, with one mighty heave, threw him right on top of the scout, who was just emerging, spluttering and screaming, from the water.

And, while the two men were still standing in the fountain, soaked, dripping and fuming with anger, Larry McLean walked out of the hotel lobby, down into the street, out of sight—and out of baseball. The Giants never saw Larry McLean again!

Another colorful receiver was Gabby Hartnett of the Cubs. He and umpire Charlie Moran used to have fun with each other. Once, protesting a close call at the plate, Hartnett howled, "You're lousing up the whole league!"

"And you're out of the ball game!" snapped Moran.

"Gee, I didn't mean anything personal," said Gabby. "I meant *all* the umpires in the league."

Another time, Gabby was working a Cubs-Reds game, with Moran peering over his shoulder as plate umpire. Up to the plate came Hughie Critz, the Reds' weak-hitting second baseman. Critz knew that Moran bred hunting dogs—and at once he brought up the subject.

"Got any good ones for sale?" he asked Moran.

"Yup, got one for a $150," said the umpire as he called ball one.

"That's a lot of money," said Critz.

"Not for the best hound dog in my kennel," said Moran, calling ball two.

"Is he fast?" said Critz.

"He'll run right past any rabbit," said the ump, and he called ball three.

"Can he retrieve?" asked Critz.

"Through fire and water," said Moran.

"I'll buy him," said Critz.

"Ball four!" called Moran, sending Critz to first.

That was too much for Hartnett. He threw off his mask and whirled on Moran. "Will you stop selling your lousy hound dogs to lousy .200 hitters!" he yelled.

Jimmy Dykes and umpire Bill McGowan were colorful scrappers, too. Jimmy didn't have any great love for umpires in general, and, because he made no bones about his feelings, he felt that the umpires, in turn, were "out to get him." McGowan, he said, was worst of all, thumbing him out of a game on the slightest pretext.

One day, a Philadelphia teammate was thrown out of a game by McGowan, "for using vile language." Dykes rushed up to McGowan, demanding to know what the player had said.

"None of your business," said McGowan, "and you're out of the game too!"

"Me? What for?" said Dykes.

"For . . . for expostulation!" said the umpire.

"Nuts!" roared Dykes. "You're just showing off. You don't even know what that big word means!"

"I don't, eh?" snarled McGowan, his pride wounded. "Well, Mr. Dykes, I know very well what it means. It means . . . holding up the game! And that's why you're out of it now!"

McGowan had a Scotsman's pride—but he also had a sense of the ridiculous, and good humor. He didn't always take himself seriously. One day, when he was umpiring a game between the White Sox and the Yankees, he was calling a lot of walks against Chicago hurler Saul Rogovin.

Rogovin was beginning to burn a bit, but every time he took a step off the mound, as though to voice a protest, McGowan would yell at him, "Get back in there and pitch, busher!"

After a number of such occasions, Rogovin lost his

temper and stalked off the mound to have it out with McGowan. He was met halfway by the umpire, who ripped off his mask and said, "Listen, busher, get back up there! You ought to pay your way into the ball park just to see me umpire."

An angry reply was on Rogovin's lips—until he saw the big grin plastered across McGowan's face. Rogovin grinned back, returned to the mound and pitched the rest of the game without protest.

One morning, McGowan was having a ham sandwich and a cup of coffee in the commissary at Yankee Stadium. It was an hour or so before game time, on a Tuesday. At that moment Mark Roth, the Yankees' road secretary, came by.

"A fine Scotsman you are," said Mark, "eating ham on a Friday."

McGowan almost choked. "What day is this?" he asked, suddenly confused.

"That's a hot one," Roth said. "Here's an umpire going to work a ball game in an hour and he doesn't even know what day it is!"

According to Harry Walker (and lots of other people around baseball), the umpires have changed, as so many others things have in baseball. Walker claims that umpires today are hypersensitive, not as tolerant as they were years ago. It used to be that a manager could get into a good argument with an umpire and not get chased unless he used bad language or was otherwise abusive— or unless the umpire felt capricious that day and decided he didn't feel like a battle of wits. In any case, arguing with the umpire was often fun, and part of the game.

Today, complained Harry, one wisecrack and you're out.

"We're playing Montreal," he explained to sportswriter Dick Young one day, "and John Kibler is working at second base. It's the first game of the series. Johnny Edwards hits one for us that goes over the yellow line we have in the Astrodome to indicate home runs.

"Kibler motions that the ball is in play. It rebounds almost to second base. I come out and say, 'For God's sake John, the ball went in and out. It hit the girder. There's no way the ball could rebound that far if it hit below the line.'

"Well, Edwards has to settle for a double, and two days later Kibler is working the game behind the plate. Edwards is up again with a man on first, and this time he hits a little spinner in front of the plate. Bateman jumps on it, figuring to throw to second, and misses it. The ball rolls off to the side, and this time Bateman gets it and throws to first. But by this time he gets nobody. But Kibler calls it a foul ball.

"I run out and say, 'How come? He says, 'Bateman didn't touch the ball the first time.' I say, 'How come it went foul?' I say, 'Bateman knocked it foul.' He says, 'It spun foul by itself.' I say, 'John, a couple days ago you couldn't see a ball 250 feet away. Tonight you can't see one under your nose. Some people are farsighted and some nearsighted, but you're both!'

"And for a little thing like that, he kicks me out!"

Walker, better known as Harry the Hat during his playing days with the Cardinals, also tells a Dusty Boggess story when he talks about the older generation of umps.

Harry liked to swing away, but one day he came to the plate with orders to take a couple of pitches before swinging. The pitcher, sniffing out the situation, popped a fast ball right over the middle. Harry kept the bat on his shoulder. The next pitch was a curve, at the knees, and Boggess called strike two.

"That looked a little low," Walker protested mildly.

Boggess chuckled. "Listen Walker, if you can take a strike for him," he said, thumbing toward the manager's spot on the bench, "then you can take one for Ol' Dusty. Now get in there and hit, 'cause you got just one left."

A great Leo Durocher–versus-the-umpire story concerns the time George Magerkurth approached him before a Dodger game and asked, "Who's your pitcher today, Leo?"

"Guess!" snapped Durocher. "That's all you did yesterday!"

Gil Hodges' record as a peace-loving manager can be matched by few major-league pilots, present or past. One of those few whose record is even better, considering how many years he managed, is Connie Mack. The late manager of the Philadelphia Athletics had no temper. He rarely lost patience with his men, even under the most trying of circumstances.

Once, in the late innings of a close game, Mack was looking for a pinch hitter on the bench, and Frank Brugge, the third-string catcher, grabbed a bat and asked for a chance to go in and belt one. Reluctantly, Mack let him have his way.

Brugge promptly popped one up to first base. As he came back to the bench, he was greeted by a bitter look from Mack, who said to him, "Next time I need a pinch hitter, Frank, don't you dare make a move!"

No one ever tried Mack's limitless patience the way Rube Waddell did. The Rube was one of the great pitching talents of his day, but he was another of those eccentric pitchers who bent his elbow at the bar more often than on the mound.

Mack thought long and hard of a way to cure Rube of the bottle—and one day he thought he had figured out a solution. He called the pitcher to his office and began a long lecture on the evils of drink.

"Liquor will ruin you, Rube," the gentle Connie said. "I've never seen the ballplayer good enough to drink and stay in the big time. Let me prove how bad alcohol is for you. I'm going to demonstrate what that horrible stuff does to your insides."

Mack put a half-filled glass of whiskey on the desk between himself and Waddell, and then took a wriggling worm from a can at his feet. "Watch closely, I want you to keep your eye on this," said Connie. He dropped the worm in the glass. The worm immediately began to squirm and jerk, then commenced to writhe slowly, more slowly, more and more slowly yet, until at last it expired. Mack raised his head from the sight and said, "There, that ought to speak for itself, doesn't it, Rube?"

"Oh sure," answered Waddell.

"All right then," said Mack, "tell me what it means."

"You're just trying to relieve my mind," said Waddell, his voice dripping gratitude. "It's sure good to know that a drinking man ain't never gonna have to worry about worms in his stummick!"

The Rube is worth a few pages in any sports book, and his tale bears repeating ad infinitum, because Rube Waddell was one of the unique clowns of baseball. As with so many clowns, too, there was a streak of sadness under-lying the Rube's zany activities, and pathos was never so very far away.

When he came up to the major leagues, Rube Waddell was a tall, barrel-chested, long-armed country boy with an arm that never tired. He was as fast a person as any-body had ever seen and, for a lefty, had excellent control.

He was a quick sensation with the Athletics. In one season he struck out 343, and he set a record over seven seasons with a total of 1,801 strike-outs. In less than a dozen seasons he won more than 200 games. Once he pitched an entire six-game series against Detroit, and won all six.

Rube was not only one of the best pitchers of his time, he was one of the most eccentric. It seemed that he pre-ferred doing almost anything to pitching. He liked to fish, chase fires, drink, clown around and do all sorts of things on the spur of the moment. And when he was overcome by one of his whims, no baseball assignment could stop him.

Several times he simply disappeared from the baseball scene to sign up with some local fire department just so he could ride the engines to fires. Often he would miss his pitching turn because he had decided to march in, or lead, a local parade.

Once, during the height of a tough pennant race, he disappeared for ten days. When he was finally traced, he was found pitching for a sand-lot team in a small fishing town. He explained that he had simply felt like going off to fish for a while. Once, poor old Connie Mack found him wrestling live alligators in a freak show for two dollars a performance. Another time, to win a small bet, he jumped out of a two-story window. Whenever he was pitching particularly well, he turned cartwheels going from the mound to the dugout.

Then, during spring training of 1912, Rube was in Hickman, Kentucky, when the river overflowed and threatened to destroy the town. Waddell volunteered to help battle the flood. For long hours he stood up to his armpits in icy water, putting sacks of sand in place to stem the rampaging waters.

Rube was never the same after that. The cold and the wet and the physical strain brought on a bronchial disorder. He became an easy victim for tuberculosis, and he quickly began to waste away. Less than two years later, still in harness and clowning to the last, Rube Waddell died.

Perhaps aptly, certainly ironically, Rube died on April 1—April Fool's Day. He was only 37. His clown act did little to tarnish his sterling record as a moundsman during his career, and Rube is now enshrined in baseball's Hall of Fame, a pitching immortal.

It might be quite a project for a psychological study—this apparent relationship between pitching and clowning. Look at the evidence! Dizzy Dean, Lefty "Goofy" Gomez, Waddell, Satch Paige—and how about Al Schacht? Once a pitcher for the Washington Senators, Al actually made a career for himself as "The Clown Prince of Baseball."

He was never much of a pitcher, really, and always was the first to admit it. He was also ready to tell stories about himself at any time. Al was always on stage. One of his best stories concerns the time he was pitching for Jersey City under manager Turkey Mike Donlin.

Schacht was sent in to relieve late in the first game of a doubleheader, with the score tied. He threw one pitch, and the enemy hitter blasted the ball out of the park to win the game.

As Al started for the dugout, a furious fan let out a string of abuse, heaping insults on Al's head—and his pitching arm. Not to be outdone, Al let the fan have it right back. A few minutes later, a big, tough-looking fellow came into the dressing room, flashed a badge and announced that he was the sheriff and was arresting Schacht for using profane and indecent language.

Manager Donlin pleaded with the man that he was short of pitchers, and begged him to let Al stay through the second game in case he was needed again in relief. After a short argument, the man agreed.

The nightcap was a wild affair. In the fifth inning, the score was tied. Desperate, Donlin once again called on Schacht to save the day. Al came on, and, as luck would have it, the first man he faced was that same big hitter who'd ruined him in the first game.

Al hitched up his trousers and threw the first pitch, and the hitter slammed this one even farther than he'd sent the first one! The hitter was just about rounding second when Donlin was out at the mound, purple-faced with fury. He paid no attention to Schacht. He stood at the mound, searching among the crowd, until he found what he wanted. Then he raised his arm and beckoned toward the box seats. "Sheriff!" he yelled. "Come down here right now and take this guy away!"

Another favorite of Al's is of the time he was pitching and Billy Evans was umpiring behind the plate. He was giving Evans the business most of the afternoon, and the umpire was taking it quietly. Then, during the latter part of the game, it began to sprinkle, and the game was held up for a bit. During the break, Evans came over and said, "Say, Schacht, have I been seeing all your stuff today? You been throwing any fast balls?"

"Are you kidding?" replied Al. "I must have thrown about a dozen of my best!"

"Ah well," said Evans, "in that case I can see I won't need this." And he let all the air out of his chest protector, deflating Al as well for the rest of the game!

More zany pitcher stories? They stretch from here to Mars. There was Jinx Poindexter, for example. One day

Jinx reported to the Phillies manager, Doc Prothro, that he had a bad toothache. The Doc, once a practicing dentist, peered into Poindexter's gaping jaws, muttered a "Hmm" and gave the lad five dollars to get the tooth seen to (the good old days of five-dollar dentistry!).

Jinx was not only flaky in the best tradition of pitchers; he was also tightfisted in that same tradition. (Joe Garagiola once said of Warren Spahn: "He could even save money in Las Vegas.")

So Jinx shopped around, and found a dentist who would yank the molar for two bucks. Now, with a little mental effort, Jinx realized that he was onto a good thing. A three-dollar profit was not to be sneered at. A week or so later, therefore, he reported another toothache to Prothro, who slipped him another five for the dentist. This went on for a few months as one after another, Poindexter's molars were sacrificed for the sake of good business.

After a while, Prothro got tired of forking over five-dollar bills, and stopped paying. But Jinx, although screwy, was no complete dope. The moment Prothro stopped paying, he stopped having toothaches!

Another pitcher with Pagliacci overtones similar to Rube Waddell's was Lefty Lee Grissom. Signed to pitch for Cincinnati, Grissom reported to the rookie camp in West Virginia, and promptly established himself as one of the looney-bin club. Lee had a really terrific fast ball, and in camp he used to warm up as often as 12 times a day, just to show off to the coal miners who came around to watch.

One afternoon, Grissom pitched, and won easily. When the game was over, he remained on the mound receiving well-wishers, shaking everyone's hand. By the time he had finished with all his admirers, his teammates had left by bus, and in his spikes and uniform Lee had to trudge over five miles of country road to get back to his hotel.

Once, after a winning game, he disappeared while still in uniform. That evening he was finally found, marching with a minstrel show in the town's main street. Another day, his arm felt a little sore. Someone told him that the great Lefty Grove once had two teeth removed in an effort to restore his "dead arm." So Grissom rushed out and had four perfectly good teeth removed to help his own arm.

At times, directly after pitching a good game, he would go on strike demanding more money. His screwy antics finally drove him right out of the big league.

Lefty Lee Grissom's sad end came just a few years later. He became involved in a tavern brawl and killed a man.

The White Sox once had a lefty rookie named Pat Caraway, who came from Gordon, Texas. Very quickly, Pat established himself as a character in the lefty pitcher mold. Early that spring, during a blustery afternoon in Chicago, Pat asked to be excused from the game.

"I gotta go home," he said to the Chisox skipper.

"What for?" demanded the manager.

"I'm cold and I forgot to bring my overcoat," Caraway said.

Figuring he would humor his rookie hurler and make him happier in the big town by letting him return to his hotel for a while, the manager said.

"Well okay, go home and get your overcoat—but don't take too long."

So zany Caraway left the Chicago ball park and went home to Gordon, Texas, to get his overcoat.

Baseball fans who go back a few years remember with tearful nostalgia the old home of the Giants, the Polo Grounds, and the colorful denizens thereof. They would remember, too, the time manager Mel Ott slapped pitcher Bill Voiselle with a $500 fine for breaking his rule against coming in with a fat pitch on an 0–2 count. The Giant pitchers, a ragged crew in any event, trod carefully from that point. And then, one day, a young pitcher, sent in to relieve, got two strikes on the hitter.

The next pitch was meant to break away wide of the plate, but instead the curve just nicked the outside corner.

"Strike three!" yelled the umpire.

The rookie pitcher was white with fear as he rushed

to the plate, "No, no!" he cried. "What are you trying to do, ruin me? That was a ball!"

Those who got to see Willie Mays break into baseball in the old Polo Grounds were lucky indeed. It was a milestone in baseball history. But it took young Willie a little while to get going. In fact, he went out 13 straight times before he got his first major-league hit.

Then the Giants went on the road. In the opener of the Pittsburgh series, they carried a 3–2 lead into the bottom of the eighth. The Pirates rallied, getting two men on base with two out. Up stepped Gus Bell, and the Pittsburgh slugger slammed a pitch to deepest center field. In Forbes Field, that's a long way indeed.

Anyway, Willie turned around and gave chase. He ran . . . and ran . . . and ran . . . and he ran some more. Then, snatching a quick look over his shoulder to locate the ball, he leaped high in the air—and actually caught the ball in his bare hand!

Willie fell down after the catch, rolling over and over, but he came up with the ball, saving the game.

The incredible catch lifted young Willie's spirits, and he loped back to the Giant bench, fully expecting the excited congratulations of his teammates and his manager. But Willie didn't know about the "silent treatment" big leaguers like to use on "fresh bushers."

When he got back to the dugout, he looked around for

some sign of praise or congratulation, but was met instead with stony indifference. Al Dark was busy tying his shoe-laces. Whitey Lockman was at the water cooler. Ed Stanky was picking a bat out of the rack. And so forth. Leo Durocher, the manager, from whom more than any-one else Willie wanted praise, was sitting and staring quietly out at the field.

Willie couldn't understand it. He couldn't believe it. He sat down on the bench next to Durocher, bursting with frustration. Still nothing was said. Finally, Willie was un-able to contain himself any longer.

"Skipper," he cried in his high, shrill voice, "Skipper, did you see me catch that ball? Did you see me catch that ball?"

At that the Giant bench broke up with laughter.

Funny things happened at the Polo Grounds. The old stadium at Coogan's Bluff seemed to bring out the comic in the strangest and most sober of people.

Once, in the course of a Dodger-Giant game, umpire Augie Donatelli gave the thumb to Bobby Thomson. Normally Thomson was a very quiet type, and so he later asked Donatelli why he had thrown him out.

"My honor was at stake," said Augie.

"Your honor!" Thomson exclaimed. "I'll bet you don't even remember what happened!"

"Yes, I do," replied the umpire. "I called a strike on you, and you called me a bad name."

"Okay," admitted Thomson, "but why did you kick me out? Only you, me and the catcher heard it."

"I know," said Augie, "but I didn't want that catcher to go through life thinking that's really what I was!"

In those days, if it didn't happen at Ebbets Field, it had to happen at the Polo Grounds. Where else could the following have happened?

Mel Ott was playing right field then, and Bill Terry was playing first and managing the club. During this particular game, Ted McGrew was umpiring behind the plate.

In the first inning McGrew called a close one against the Giants, and Terry began to burn, slowly. In the third inning McGrew did it again, and Terry beefed loudly. McGrew did it again in the fifth, and again in the seventh. Terry exploded. He rushed in from first base, yelling at the plate umpire, ranting and raging and kicking up dirt in front of him.

Ott ran in from right field to calm Terry, just in time to hear McGrew shout, "Terry, you're out of the game!"

"You can't put me out!" Terry protested. "I don't have anybody else to play first base!"

McGrew thought for a moment, then whirled on Ott. "Okay then, you—Ott *you're* out of the game!"

Take Two and Hit to Right

It turned out to be the first and *only* time lovable Mel Ott was ever thrown out of a ball game.

Even old Casey Stengel was part of the historic Giants scene. Case, who seems to have been just about everywhere as a player and manager, spent a couple of seasons as an outfielder under John McGraw. And he was just as funny then as he was many years later managing the Yankees and the Mets.

One spring the Giants came to a small town in the deep South to play an exhibition game. That afternoon, Casey was truly something else. He hit three home runs, made a number of sensational catches and even stole a couple of bases. But he heard few cheers, for just a few dozen people turned out to see the ball game. That night, the town council threw a welcoming banquet to honor the visiting big leaguers, and the town's leading citizens and dignitaries crowded the dining room.

Finally the coffee came, and Stengel was called upon to say a few words. He rose and said:

"It's nice to see so many of you here tonight. But where in blazes were all you lazy bums this afternoon when you could have seen me play some real ball?"

Casey holds the distinction of being the only ballplayer in history to pay $300 for a haircut and a shave. It happened, of course, during those Giant days.

Fabulous John McGraw had the knack of taking a

101

strange assortment of characters and molding them into pennant winners. McGraw won ten pennants during his reign, but it was a battle every inch of the way—not only against the other teams in the league but also against all the temptations luring his men away from the straight and narrow.

If there was any one thing McGraw hated above all others, it was the sight of a drunken ballplayer. One afternoon before an important game, McGraw got his players together in the locker room and began an angry talk. The object lesson of his harangue was one member of the team who had appeared earlier that afternoon for practice— and in a slightly tipsy condition. McGraw was waxing eloquent on the evils of drink, and had just reached the climax of his speech by slapping a fine on the offender, when suddenly, into the locker room swaggered Casey Stengel.

He was late, because he had just come from the barber shop, where he had gotten "the works." His hair was trimmed and neatly plastered down, and his freshly shaven face was sprinkled and lacquered with a liberal dose of a lotion popular at the time—bay rum. The smell of that bay rum instantly assaulted McGraw's nostrils. It was like waving a red flag at an angry bull.

Seething, McGraw walked up to his outfielder, sniffed and snorted around him for a moment or two, then roared, "You too? How dare you show up smelling from drink?

You no good drunken tramp—I'm fining you a hundred bucks!"

When the shocked—and quite innocent—Stengel found his voice, he said, "You're out of your head, Mac. I didn't touch a drop!"

An even angrier McGraw roared back. "All right, Casey, and there's another hundred-buck fine for lying to me!"

Now it was Casey's turn to explode. He roared in turn, "You're blind and you're crazy, Mac! I don't care what you say . . ."

McGraw, in complete fury, interrupted him: "And it'll cost you another hundred for insubordination!"

That ended the argument. Casey saw it could cost him still more in McGraw's mood, so he shut up and paid— $300 for a haircut, a shave and a sprinkling of bay rum!

That's baseball for you, a uniquely colorful game— especially when it was played by two of the most unique and colorful teams in baseball annals, the New York Giants and the Brooklyn Dodgers. During one such contest years ago, as manager Durocher for Brooklyn was squeezing 18 men into the game and manager Ott 17 for the Giants, a press-box observer remarked, "I'd hate to have to explain this game to an Englishman."

Replied his neighbor, "I'd hate to have to explain this game to an American!"

WHEN in DOUBT, PUNT!

In the rugged world of football, the niceties of life are not always well observed. Players and coaches alike, caught up in the competitive spirit, develop a thick coat of toughness. But they need it to survive. One of the toughest of them all was the late Vince Lombardi, a coach of Napoleonic ego and talents. Lombardi was tougher than any Marine drill instructor, and was not exactly famous for coddling his players. Once, when he was coaching the Packers, a member of the city council cornered him at a testimonial dinner and said, "Coach, you're doing a fine job, but how is it the players don't seem to love you the way players on other teams love their coaches?"

Lombardi grunted and replied, gruffly, "I guess I've been too busy coaching to do any courting!"

The coach, of course, usually gets blamed when his team loses—that comes with the job. But sometimes catching the blame can be an exasperating—and amusing —experience. Bud Wilkinson liked to tell of the time his Oklahoma team was losing to Notre Dame because it kept fumbling the ball away. Time after time, golden scoring chances were lost because the offense couldn't hold onto the ball. At the half the Irish were leading, 21–0. When Oklahoma came out for the second half, the players had to wait on the steps for a few moments as the Oklahoma band completed its routine on the field. Just then the Oklahoma drum major threw his baton in the air; when it came down, he missed it.

A nearby Oklahoma partisan shouted out: "Hey Wilkinson, I see you coach the band too!"

Such lack of sympathy extends even to the coach's friends and family. Eddie Erdelatz remembers one disastrous year, coaching Navy, when the Middies won only two games out of ten, then upset Army, 14–2, and got a rousing parade through the streets of Annapolis. Erdelatz had his young son with him during the parade. At one point the boy turned and said to him, "What's everybody so happy about, Dad—have they forgotten all those games you lost?"

The exasperation of a football coach was colorfully expressed in midseason recently by Missouri football coach Dan Devine.

When in Doubt, Punt!

"When the season's over," he said, "I'm going to put a football under my arms and head south. I'll cross the border into Mexico and keep going until somebody asks me, 'What's that thing under your arm?' That's where I'm going to stop, check into a hotel and rest for a few days."

Buddy Parker, who coached the Steelers many years ago through a series of unhappy seasons, was known for his waspish wit. One awful Sunday afternoon, when quarterback Bobby Layne had thrown seven straight passes without a connection, Parker greeted him back at the bench with: "Layne, if it wasn't for the law of gravity, you couldn't even hit the ground!"

One of the great and truly beloved coaches of all time was Knute Rockne of Notre Dame. His Fighting Irish teams of the 1920s were so good that other coaches often thought it a privilege even to be scheduled by Notre Dame. One such coach was John McEwan of Army. Before one Army–Notre Dame game, whose outcome was a foregone conclusion, the two coaches met at midfield. Said Rockne: "Mac, how about limiting the game today to four 12-minute periods?"

"Nothing doing!" replied McEwan. "I'm expecting 60 minutes of instruction out of Notre Dame, and you're not going to cheat me out of 12 minutes!"

Although Rockne was of Norwegian ancestry, for some reason he was known as "The Swede." He was an agile verbal dueler who delighted in exchanging ripostes with players and reporters. Once, however, he was bested by one of his own men. During a workout, Sleepy Jim Crowley was having trouble getting a blocking assignment right, and Rockne growled at him, "Crowley, can you name anyone dumber than a dumb Irishman?"

"Sure," retorted Crowley, "a smart Swede!"

Crowley could get away with it, of course, because he was a great star at Notre Dame, a terrific running back. He was, however, not overly modest, and this enabled Rockne to get his own back in another verbal duel.

Against Princeton one day, Crowley broke into the open and seemed headed for a touchdown. But he began to showboat a bit, and the Princeton safety, Slagle, nabbed him from behind on the ten-yard line.

In the locker room during the half, Crowley apologized to Rockne. "Sorry, Coach," he said. "I made a mistake. I didn't know Slagle was that fast. I should have cut back."

"That wasn't your mistake," said Rockne.

"Yes, it was," Crowley insisted. "I admit it. I should have cut back."

"No," said Rockne, "it was just that Slagle didn't know who you were. If you'd have shown him all those clippings you've been saving, he wouldn't have dared come near you!"

Hunk Anderson, Rockne's line coach, combined with Knute to make a delightful combination. While Hunk would be working with the guards and tackles, Rockne would handle the ends and backs. When he was ready for a scrimmage, Rockne would call out to Hunk, using his given name:

"Hearley, old fellow, would you mind bringing the behemoths over here?"

Anderson would go right on working, and Rockne would call again. "Hearley, would you mind bringing your monsters over for a few minutes?"

Again no response from Anderson, and so Rockne would call a third time. Finally Hunk would yell, "Wait a few minutes, yet, Rock. These guys ain't even bleedin' yet!"

One favorite Rockne story concerns his experience with soccer. For a time he was convinced it was a good conditioner, and he introduced it into preseason training. Describing the game, he said, "The idea in soccer is either to kick the ball or kick the other fellow's shins."

Some of his players didn't share his enthusiasm. One day he lined them up for practice, when they discovered they had no ball. After a moment, one of the big guards grunted, "Aah, the heck with the ball, Coach. Let's start the game!"

Once Rockne was asked to define the perfect football player. After pondering for a few moments, he said, "I'd say the perfect football player would be a left halfback who was cross-eyed and could pass with either hand."

The rivalry among college coaches for good young high school players is well known. Stories about the scouting and recruiting of strong young lads have all the cloak-and-dagger aspects of spy novels. A coach's greatest delight is the "stealing" of a fine prospect from under the nose of one of his rivals.

If a coach couldn't actually beat a rival to the punch, his next greatest delight would be in making him think so, at least.

When Herman Hickman was line coach at North Carolina State, he paid a visit one night to the home of Peahead Walker, then coach at Wake Forest. As soon as he had taken off his coat, Hickman began bragging about a tackle he had just recruited for State.

"He's the best tackle in all of North Carolina," bragged Hickman. "And he's mine, all mine!"

"Who is this boy?" asked Peahead.

Hickman was so sure he had the boy all sewn up that he answered, "Pat Preston from Roanoke Orphanage."

"Him!" exclaimed Peahead. Then he whispered. "Better talk softly about that boy."

"What for?" said Hickman. "Why can't I brag about some boy I got for myself!"

"Well, I'll tell you," said Peahead, softly, "Preston is upstairs right now. He's living with me just like he was my own son. And if he hears you talking about him like that, why he's just liable to get a big head!"

Coaches and their quarterbacks make good story material. When the great Slingin' Sammy Baugh came to the Redskins from Texas Christian University, he bumped up against Coach Ray Flaherty, who showed no mercy to rookie quarterbacks. In a scrimmage one day, Flaherty worked out a play. "You," he said, pointing to one of the ends, "you go downfield and buttonhook behind the middle linebacker. And you, Baugh, you got to get away a fast throw there. And I want you to hit your man right in the eye with that pass, you hear!"

"Sure, Coach," Baugh replied calmly. "Which eye?"

Joe Namath's sense of humor hasn't always appealed to his coaches, or to some of the Jets' fans. But veteran NFL official Tommy Bell tells of a good-humored exchange he had with Joe during the 1969 Super Bowl.

At one point, with the Jets leading, Namath said to him, "Mr. Bell, for a National League official, you're doing a pretty good job." To which Bell retorted, "Don't congratulate me—my team is behind."

AFL official John McDonald can also attest to Joe's sense of humor during a game. Once, after throwing an incomplete pass, Joe rushed up to McDonald, officiating on the Jet's side of the line, and said, "John, run down there and call that. You saw that interference."

Since the incompletion had come on third down, Joe left the field with the offensive unit. The next time the Jets got the ball, McDonald went over to talk to Namath. "You know, Joe, it's my job to protect the quarterback against rough stuff. But the next time you pass, I'll go downfield to make sure your receivers aren't interfered with. So you take good care of yourself back there."

"Now wait a minute," said Joe. "On second thought, you better stay here and take care of me. Let those other guys watch out for themselves!"

The bane of all quarterbacks, but especially any flinger with weak legs, like Joe's, is a blitzing linebacker. One of the most ferocious of all of these, Mike Curtis, earned a reputation with Baltimore as being absolutely merciless. Sports writers termed him "a ruthless beast who delights in knocking down quarterbacks."

Fed up one day, Curtis told one of them, "What would really be a kick for me would be to go up to the next sports writer who asks me if I'm really an animal and bite him on the arm!"

During the heat and fury of a game, players *have* been known to bite each other, of course. Which brings to mind part of a speech made years ago by Jimmy Conzelman, when he was coaching at Washington University. Conzelman, a witty afterdinner speaker, was replying to a newspaper's charge that the connection between morals and college athletics was dubious, and that college football players were taught that anything, even slugging, was right when done for alma mater.

"That report is right," said Conzelman, sardonically, "although we at Washington don't teach slugging. Our teams aren't big enough. But biting—now biting we find very effective. Biting doesn't need size, and certainly not much speed. One of the finest guards I ever coached was Biter Jones, with a splendid undershot jaw that gave him an advantage once he got hold. He had a great record at Washington. Besides making the All-Star Team, Biter Jones bit 11 guards, two centers and a flanker back. He only lost 65 yards through penalties. The only criticism he ever got was when the Sigma Chi fraternity broke his pledge for snapping at a house mother!"

Not all the monsters of the front line are vicious. Tough, yes, but not vicious. Some in fact are gentle men.

Bob St. Clair, who played tackle for the 49ers under coach Frankie Albert, was a six-foot-nine 265-pounder who had to be needled constantly by Albert in order to reach any sort of emotional pitch. During one of St. Clair's meeker Sunday afternoons, Albert grabbed the big tackle on the sidelines and sneered, "Why you pantywaist, if I were as big as you I'd be heavyweight champion of the world!"

St. Clair looked down on the five-nine Albert and replied, "Oh yeah? Then why aren't you the lightweight champion?"

Eddie LeBaron, who quarterbacked the Redskins at one time, used to get his share of ribbing, too, because of his small size. He tells the story of when he was still playing for the College of the Pacific, and was on a train with the team, heading for a game in Chicago against Northwestern. The team was walking in file through the train, heading for the diner, when the line stopped next to two elderly ladies. Little Eddie was sandwiched between a six-foot-four, 260-pound tackle and a six-five, 250-pound end.

"Who are those big men?" said one lady to the other.

"A football team," came the reply. "They're going to Chicago to play Northwestern."

"How nice," said the first lady. "And one of them is taking his little boy to the game."

When in Doubt, Punt!

LeBaron also gets in on the biting stories. Once asked if he found defensive teams to be playing dirtier football than offensive teams, he said, "Oh no! You must understand that those boys have to defend themselves against me. After all, they're only about six-four or six-five and weigh maybe 260. I remember once I went back to pass and big Len Ford came at me. I tried to stiff-arm him, and my hand went through his face mask. And he bit me! Served me right for attacking him, didn't it!"

Needless to say, the physical toll pro football takes of a man is a heavy one. Commented Jets' lineman Dave Herman about it: "When I get to be 40, I'm going to charge people just to watch me get out of bed!"

Such an active life, of course, makes big eaters out of those mammoth pro players—eaters who could more than challenge some of the famous knife-and-forkers of baseball. Bob St. Clair was one, although he was known more for style than for quantity. One story is of the time St. Clair entered a restaurant and ordered a steak. The waiter asked how he liked it.

"Raw," said St. Clair.

"You mean blood rare?" said the waiter.

"I mean raw," repeated St. Clair. "Bring it just the way they cut it off the cow."

The waiter tried again. "Should I put it under the fire just a little?"

"Look!" roared St. Clair, "just take that meat out of the icebox and put it on a plate!"

The quantity champion of today's game, however, seems to be Steve Chomysak of the Bengals. The story told about Steve is that he went into one of those all-you-can-eat restaurants in Cincinnati one night and began chomping away. According to teammates, he put away 15 lobsters, eight dozen shrimp, a platter of six different kinds of fish, two pounds of roast beef, two bottles of wine and two whole pies. He was just looking around for more when the restaurant owner came over and tapped him on the shoulder.

"You're our guest," he said. "No check. Just leave— now!"

Don Shula, coach of the Dolphins, was trying to explain confidence one day to quarterback Bob Griese. Shula told of the day he was out duck hunting with quarterback Len Dawson.

They waited for an hour. No ducks. Finally one solitary duck came winging over, high and fast. Dawson took a shot. The duck kept going.

Said Dawson, "Don, you are seeing a true miracle. There flies a dead duck."

When in Doubt, Punt!

That, explained Shula to Griese, is confidence.

Another Dawson story is the one Dawson tells about himself, when he was a youngster. Len grew up in Alliance, Ohio, and he and his seven brothers were all hot Cleveland Indians fans. For Sunday doubleheaders he and the rest of the family would pile into two station wagons and go off to Cleveland. Once, after such a doubleheader, the Dawson tribe piled back into the wagons and headed for home—leaving Len behind in the stadium!

Poor Len, loitering behind to go to the men's room, had become lost in the shuffle. Obviously, the Dawsons in each station wagon thought Len was in the other one!

Len sniffled and snuffled around the stadium for a long time, wondering what to do, when he suddenly realized he had just enough silver in his pocket to dial the operator and call home collect.

His parents wired some money at once to the stadium office, and little Len finally staggered home about three o'clock the next morning!

Joe Namath's white shoes are his trademark, but so in a lesser way are the cleats of Warren Wells, wide receiver for Oakland. Wells tapes his regular shoes white. When asked why, he replied, "So I'll look good if they have to carry me off the field!"

The 1970 season was a particularly unhappy one for coach John Rauch of the Buffalo Bills. And they weren't all player problems, either. During one late-season game against the Colts, Rauch had cause to grieve over the officiating. Buffalo lost 103 yards in penalties, against only five for Baltimore. Once, the officials reversed a first-down decision, allowing the Colts to keep the ball instead of forcing them to punt out. On another occasion, 12 Colts were on the field, but the infraction went undetected.

All of which had Rauch in an unfriendly mood when the reporters came around to interview him after the game. After a few routine questions, one sports writer asked, "Say, John, who will the Bills be going for in the pro draft this year?"

Said Rauch: "We may trade our first pick for two good game officials."

Blustery Larry MacPhail was well known for his temper around baseball circles. But once he stuck his nose in on a football rivalry—and almost had it snapped off by a fabulous old gridiron wit. It happened during the Army–Notre Dame game, back in 1946. Just before game time, coach Frank Leahy was giving his Fighting Irish a pep talk. The tension in the locker room was terrific; the Army–Notre Dame contest was one of the big traditional rivalries in college football.

In the middle of Leahy's spiel, the door was flung open and in walked MacPhail.

Leahy jumped at him. "What do you want?" he demanded. "You can't come in here!"

"The heck I can't!" shouted MacPhail. "I'm Larry MacPhail, and I own this ball park!"

"Is that so?" sneered Leahy. "Then come back tomorrow. We rented the place for today!"

MacPhail, of course, was just doing what any rabid football fan would do, given the chance. Fans are famous for doing strange things to get close to their idols. Comedian Phil Foster went to one extreme during a recent summer—and found the experience as painful as it was enjoyable.

A great Chicago Bear fan, Phil asked the Bears' management if he could come on field while the team was going through its practice scrimmages.

He was told he could, but he'd have to sign a contract. Phil signed on for one dollar, and was allowed to be part of the "chain gang," working the ten-yard markers. His partner was another one-dollar-contract player, Joe Kellerman, a Chicago businessman.

Soon after the scrimmage began, there was a fake to Gale Sayers, and a give to Brian Piccolo. The big back headed for the sidelines, toward the chain gang. Hot in pursuit were half a dozen giant defenders.

Foster and Kellerman froze. They didn't want to drop the chains and run—or maybe they did, but were rooted to the spot by the sight of some half a ton of muscle and bone bearing down on them.

The two men began yelling—things like "Stop!" and "Help!"

They were still yelling when Piccolo and a horde of defense men ran right over them.

Favoring the offensive squad, Foster and Kellerman began cheating a bit on the yardage. They might have got away with it if Foster had been able to repress his instincts for farce. He was caught when he called out, in his Brooklyn accent, "Foist and eight!"

The defenders squawked loudly. "Hey, you don't know what the heck you're doing!" shouted the defensive captain.

"Shaddup!" yelled Foster. "Who's holding the chain here, me or you? I said foist and eight! Play ball!"

Officials in football take their share of abuse, as do the officials in all sports. Sometimes it is deserved, sometimes not. Making decisions on the spur of the moment, in the heat of a contest, isn't easy. Sound judgment is needed—sometimes, the wisdom of a Solomon.

For example, during a Wake Forest–Clemson game recently, a pass was thrown that caused a difference of opinion among the officials. One ruled it a completion, one ruled it an interception and one admitted he had been blocked out and couldn't see the play.

When in Doubt, Punt!

Referee Jack Lindsay solved the problem by calling it incomplete. "What else could you call it?" he explained. "A jump ball?"

The artificial turf used by the University of Texas football team may be easy on the players, but, according to *Sport* magazine columnist Bob Rubin, it's tough on the grasshoppers. Rubin reports a conversation with Bill Ellington, assistant athletic director at Texas.

"I've seen two or three grasshoppers out here," said Ellington, "and they don't know what to do. They're the most frustrated things. You come back the next day and they'll be lying there, dead. I don't know whether they die of shock or what!"

Veteran defensive tackle Jim Hunt of the Boston Patriots is the subject of a story that has been making the rounds of the pro gridirons. In the off-season, Jim took a job as a security man in a plant doing government work. Anyone coming through the gate had to show identification. On Jim's second day at the job, the president of the company showed up at the gate. As luck would have it, the man had no proper identification. Hunt stopped him. At first the president was angry; then, after he had rounded up some men to vouch for him, he thought it over and praised Hunt for his dedication. But he did wonder why he hadn't been recognized.

"You must be a new guard," said the president.

"No," replied Jim, "I'm just an old tackle!"

One of the more irreverent football players of years past was Buddy Dial. Nobody was safe from his flippant tongue. Once in a while he would come close to overstepping the bounds. At a dinner in Cleveland one time, he was needling Steelers teammate Bob Ferguson, saying his laziness had hurt the club.

"One thing I'm sure of," Buddy said. "If there was an Olympic sleeping team, Fergie would be on it."

It got back to Dial that Woody Hayes, who had coached Ferguson at Ohio State, was incensed at the remark, which had been quoted in the papers. So the next time he was called upon to speak at a dinner, Dial's opening remark was: "Hey, I just found out Woody Hayes can read."

Still not suppressed, but anxious to avoid an incident, Dial followed up with: "But really, Fergie's an improved player. Last year all he knew was one play. This year he knows two!"

Then he added, "I'm only kidding!"

The day of the less-than-six-footer is just about gone in pro football, and in fact the giants have been taking over gradually for years. Some time back, Billy Butler, a Viking halfback, was considered the midget of the team, though he stood five-foot-ten. Norm Van Brocklin, who coached the team then, used to say Butler was the only man in football who had to high-jump the chalk marks on the field.

Once, when he stood on the scales in the dressing room, a teammate yelled, "Hey, Butler, that's the first time I've seen your knees this season—they ain't been cutting the grass out there much and all I get to see of you is from the waist up!"

A New York sports writer asked Phil Silvers, the comic, who he had picked as Super Bowl champs for the 1970-71 season. "The Jets," said Silvers, sadly.

"Me too," said the sports writer.

Said Silvers, "I'm a comedian—what's your excuse?"

The Jets history is in fact a strange and checkered one. When Weeb Ewbank ran the club, he had the men pray before and after every game. Once, after they had dropped a close contest, the reporters headed for the clubhouse, only to be stopped at the door by the water man. "Not now," he said, "the Jets is praying."

"Say," joked one writer, "there might be an atheist in there being embarrassed to pray against his will." He reminded the water man about the Supreme Court edict regarding prayer in schools.

"The Supreme Court ain't got no say in the matter,"

the water man retorted. "This ain't no public school. The Jets prays when they wants!"

Willie Townes is a murderous defense man—a bone crusher. And, like a lot of big men, he has a wistful sense of humor. After one game, he was asked why he had dived on running back Donny Anderson even though the whistle had already blown.

"I know it looked as though the guy's motion had been stopped," explained Willie, "but he was still moving his eyebrows, so I flopped on him."

Pleasant-faced Willie (off the field, that is) was once asked how he managed to wake up each morning with a smile, no matter what.

"Easy," he quipped. "I go to bed with a coat hanger in my mouth."

Johnny Unitas can also throw a gag around—aside from the football, that is. One Sunday afternoon, before a Colts game, he was supposed to throw autographed footballs into the stands for a charity contest. He had been having a succession of poor games before that day, and so remarked, "Maybe I better just hand 'em off!"

Tall stories abound in football, on and off the field. Publicists help create and develop legends about players.

When in Doubt, Punt!

One year Bob Cheyne, pounding out publicity for the University of Arkansas, sent out a press release saying that end Jim John's football experience had come in handy while he was out hunting one day. Apparently John emptied his rifle at a deer, missed and finally brought the buck down with a flying tackle. Then he sat on the hapless animal until it died.

When Bo McMillin was quarterbacking the famous "Praying Colonels" of Centre College, he fell into disfavor with his coach, Charley Moran. Saturday came around, and Bo was still in the doghouse. In the third quarter, with Centre trailing, the fans began shouting, "We want Bo!"

After several minutes of the chanting, Moran motioned to McMillin. Bo ripped off his jacket and ran over. "Who do I go in for?" he asked Moran.

"You're not going *in,* you're going *up!*" the coach said, motioning toward the stands. "Your friends want you more than I do!"

One of the grandest old men of football coaching was Lou Little of Columbia. Lou was a true gentlemen and a fine coach. Once he tried to make a sportsmanlike gesture, but the game's officials ignored him. During this particular game, against Penn, Lou noticed that somehow his Lions had 12 men on the field. He tried to call time,

127

to point out the infraction, but the officials took no notice. Meanwhile, however, Penn ran off two plays against the 12-man team, and scored a touchdown!

On the sidelines, Lou sighed. "What bothers me most now," he said to his assistant, "is that the boys lined up 6–2–2–2, instead of 7–3–2!"

Football, as everyone knows, is playe ..ı any kind of weather—burning hot, freezing cold, rain and snow. Two winters ago Sonny Jurgensen got off a good crack on a Sunday plagued by freezing, pouring rain. The field was a quagmire as the officials tossed the game-opening coin. Sonny won the toss.

"Do we really have to play in this flood?" asked Sonny.

"Of course," said the official impatiently. "Now come on, which side do you want?"

"In that case we'll kick with the tide," replied Sonny.

The newspapers will report now and again about a football player's getting into trouble for breaking team rules, like missing curfew or having an extra beer. Such discipline was not too well known in the old days of pro football, when it was more of a ragtag sport than it is today. Then there was a football Brooklyn Dodgers as well as a baseball Brooklyn Dodgers, and it was difficult to choose between the two for daffiness and color—or, for that matter, inept performances. But laughs abounded.

When in Doubt, Punt!

In those days, the football Dodgers trained out at Freeport, Long Island. It was up to each man to find a room in a boardinghouse somewhere, so bed checks were impossible. Naturally this led to some interesting night life among the players. Dr. Ray Sweeney, who trained the Dodgers then, liked to tell his favorite story about one particular night. It went like this:

"Ace Parker and I decided to celebrate something or other one night, so we drove over to Sheepshead Bay in Brooklyn. There was a bar and grill built out over the water, and Ace and I went in. Well, before long Ace and the owner get into some argument over a game they were playing. Finally, they made a bet, and said the loser had to dive into the bay. Of course, Ace lost.

"It was probably a nice place in the summer, but this was late Autumn and the windows were closed. Now, Ace was the whole club. I couldn't let him dive in and get pneumonia or something. So they opened a window, and into Sheepshead Bay I went instead, clothes and all!

"For years I shivered every time I drove past that place," Sweeney recounted.

Stories about the hapless rookie in pro football are almost as numerous as they are in baseball. Coach Paul Brown's favorite story is of the time he sent one of his prize draft selections into the defensive backfield for the first time. On the next play the split end faked him out, grabbed the pass and scampered off for a touchdown.

On the bench later, Brown said to his star rookie: "Why didn't you watch that guy like I told you to?"

The rookie replied, "I did, coach, and he's the best I've ever seen!"

Roman Gabriel's rookie year at North Carolina State was a memorable one. Especially memorable was a moment in a game against Georgia Tech. While getting off a long pass, he was hit hard by two Engineers and dumped. As he staggered to his feet, dazed, he saw the State doctor rushing on field from the bench. Gabriel waved him off, indicating he was all right. Then, to the delight of the huge crowd, Roman proceeded to call a huddle with the Georgia Tech players!

Sonny Jurgensen remembers a funny one that happened to him in his rookie year of quarterbacking Duke. In the huddle, he suddenly realized he had 12 men on the field. Advising his Blue Devils of the infraction, he said, "Now listen, I'm gonna call a wide end sweep. When we get near our bench, one of you guys just sort of disappear and sit down."

Sonny called the play, and naturally there was a huge swarm of flying bodies around the Duke bench moments later.

Satisfied, Sonny called a huddle again—and made another unsettling discovery. He had lost three men!

When in Doubt, Punt!

The toughness of pro football today and pro football players is exemplified in this story from Bob Griese. It might be a bit apocryphal, as are a fair share of sports stories, but it's close enough to the truth to be true enough. When Don Shula took over as coach in 1970, he gave the boys a big pep talk before the Raiders game. "This is it, do or die," said Shula. "Only a dead man comes out of this game."

Early in the second period one of the Dolphins was knocked cold. Shula sent in a substitute. The man ran onto the field, and then quickly dashed back to the bench.

"Too early, coach," he said to Shula. "The guy's still breathing."

Brawn doesn't mean automatic superiority in football. When Hank Stram was coaching at Purdue some years ago, his monster crew of Boilermakers was beaten by an outweighed but smart team from Ohio State. After the loss a sympathetic friend was trying to console Stram.

"Remember," the friend said, "that in life brains usually win out against mere strength."

"Yeah?" said Stram. "Well, I'll get in the ring with Albert Einstein any day!"

Speaking of "cheering up" incidents recalls to mind a meeting between Football Commissioner Pete Rozelle and Art Modell, NFL president, after the 1969 Super

Bowl. The shock of the Jets' upset victory over the Colts had not yet passed, and Rozelle was trying to cheer Modell.

"Look at it this way," he said. "It's really good for pro football. It's probably the best thing that could have happened to all of us."

"Do you really believe that?" said Modell.

"Of course," said Rozelle. "Now that the leagues have reached parity in the public eye, it will have tremendous advantages in terms of their merger."

Modell didn't appear convinced, so Rozelle kept trying. "Look," he continued. "You got to count our blessings. The crowd got a good show, all the people watching television got a good show, the field was in good shape. Why, we were so lucky, remember, that it rained before the game and after the game, but not during the game!"

Modell looked thoughtful. "Maybe it should have rained during the game," he said. "They say rain is a great equalizer."

The Colts were overwhelming favorites in that Super Bowl contest. They looked like sure winners—on paper. After the upset, the Jets were celebrating in the clubhouse, and Matt Snell called out to coach Weeb Ewbank, "Hey, coach, when do we get our money?"

Before Ewbank could answer (the Jets were due some $15,000 per man for the victory) Gerry Philbin piped up.

When in Doubt, Punt!

"It might be a while before we get it. Rozelle's gonna have to take the Baltimore names off all the checks!"

A choice afterdinner football story is worth retelling here. The referee paced out a ten-yard penalty against the offensive team.

"What's this for?" asked the team's captain.

"Coaching from the sidelines," said the referee.

"But I thought that's a 15-yard penalty," said the captain.

"It is," said the referee. "But the kind of coaching you've been getting isn't worth that much."

This story comes from the Giants' running back Ron Johnson. It's about the eight-year-old who'd just won a place on his sand-lot football team. His father asked, "And what position do you play."

"I'm not sure yet," the boy replied. "But I heard the coach say I'd probably be the team's main drawback."

With all the money being thrown around as bonuses to future superstars graduating from the universities, the story inevitably got started that one such bonus quarterback got so much to sign he also insisted on an unlisted number on his jersey!

The City College of New York gave up trying to field a football team many years ago. High school lads who could play football went to schools that offered them football scholarships; CCNY didn't offer any. As a result, year after year, Beaver football teams were worse than terrible. After one particular 35–0 Saturday drubbing, some of the students dropped into a nearby coffee shop for refreshment. An out-of-towner, who had seen the game, approached the group.

"Your boys didn't even come close to scoring today," he said. "But I suppose they do score from time to time."

"I wouldn't know," said one of the CCNY students. "I've only been here three years."

When Tucker Frederickson was signed for a tidy sum by the New York Giants, he was interviewed by a sportscaster on a Memphis TV station. "According to mah figures, Tucker," said the sportscaster, "y'all gonna wind up earnin' more money this year than the Governor of Tennessee."

"Why not?" replied Frederickson. "I'd like to see *him* charge head first into that Baltimore line!"

Bart Starr says this happened to him, and he's such a nice fellow, who would want to doubt him?

He had suffered through a terrible game. He'd hit only ten of 25 passes, fumbled twice and been decked by charging defense men three times for lost yardage. The Packers were beaten. Bart dressed slowly, and was the last to leave the stadium. Outside, the streets were deserted, except for one little boy, who stood near the players' entrance, clutching a piece of paper.

Bart smiled. A loyal fan. "You want my autograph, son?" he asked.

"No," said the lad. "You gave it to me last week, now I'm giving it back."

One season, when Craig Morton was suffering from injuries, he sat out one Sunday at home, watching the Cowboys on the road. With him in the living room was some of his family. Midway through the second period, a neighbor's wife came in, gushing greetings.

"What's the score?" she said, though she knew nothing about football.

Sighed Craig: "Nothing—nothing."

"Oh goody," said the woman, "then I haven't missed anything yet!"

Bob Hayes, the Olympic sprint champion, has earned his reputation as the fastest man in football. Bob Riggle, who played safety for Atlanta against Hayes, once said of him: "That Hayes is so fast he can switch off the light at the bedroom doorway and be in bed before it gets dark!"

When Len Dawson first came to pro football, he was a first-round draft choice of the Steelers. But coach Buddy

Parker was not impressed with his qualities, least of all his potential as a team leader. One of Parker's assistant coaches, however, stood up for Dawson, explaining away his lack of aggressiveness by saying, "The thing is, Coach, Dawson is a very modest guy."

"Yeah?" grunted the unconvinced Parker. "Well, he's got a lot to be modest about!"

The late Vince Lombardi was a coach who believed in hammering away at the basic essentials. And, when it seemed to him his boys were getting a little lax in tackling and blocking drills, he would gather them around and start lecturing them as though they were indeed his classroom children.

Once, when his Green Bay Packers were loafing around the practice field, he called them together and, sulking, began one of these famous lectures. He held up the pigskin and began:

"Boys, this is a football, and . . ."

Came a voice from the rear: "Wait a minute, Coach, not so fast!"

Football European style, better known as soccer in this country, never really has caught on here as a spectator sport. Ralph Wilson, owner of the Buffalo Bills, found out the hard way. Some time ago he bought a share in the Detroit soccer team. He went to his first game and, at half-time, left the stadium and hailed a cab, just outside Tiger Stadium.

"What's the score?" said the driver.

"It's 1–1," replied Wilson.

"Who's pitching?" asked the driver, and Wilson knew he'd had it with his soccer team. It is now defunct.

Another soccer story, this time on the lighter side of the serious Catholic-Protestant rivalry in Northern Ireland. An Englishman from London journeyed to Belfast one day to see a football match between a team composed of Catholics play a team of Protestants. When the Catholic team scored, the Englishman shouted, "Well done!" A few minutes later, the Protestant team scored. The Englishman leaped up again and shouted, "Good show!"

This was too much for a crusty old Irishman sitting next to him. "My God, man," he said in disgust, "have you no religion at all?"

Fans of European football claim that their game is rougher than American-style football. The point is arguable, but certainly pro and college football today, rough as it is, was in many ways rougher in the old days before two-platooning and unlimited substitutions.

Alex Karras, for example, was coached by Forest Evashevski at the University of Iowa. Alex was tough, but Evashevski, who played blocking halfback to Tom Harmon at Michigan, told him a story about how tough it was when *he* played college ball.

Michigan was playing arch-rival Minnesota this particular Saturday. The knocks were coming hard and in ever-increasing numbers. Injured players were carried out, then shuffled back in again as soon as they could walk.

In the Minnesota line was a youngster who had more courage than brawn, and was taking a fearful beating. By the time the fourth quarter rolled around, the poor fellow was a mass of cuts and bruises. There came another power play right at him, and the little guy was bowled over and trampled.

This time the Minnesota coach sent word in for the lineman to come out for a breather. He staggered to his feet and wavered over to the Michigan bench, where he sat down.

"Hey you," barked the Michigan coach, "you made a mistake. This is the Michigan bench!"

"It's no mistake," said the battered player, "I came over here so they wouldn't find me!"

The Big Ten has given pro football some of its most formidable players. From Minnesota came one of the most feared fullbacks of all time—Bronko Nagurski. Bronko also cut his teeth on 60-minute football, and he became an awesome figure as he plowed through opposing teams for the old Chicago Bears.

When in Doubt, Punt!

One Sunday afternoon, after 50 minutes of body-battering football against the Redskins, Bronko was aroused to a fighting pitch nearer to complete rage. He was like a bull that had been tormented in the ring. He was bruised and frustrated by a tougher-than-usual Redskin team.

"This time," he said to himself, as he lined up on his own 30-yard line, "nothing's going to stop me. Those Skins better watch themselves!"

Nagurski took the ball on the direct pass from center, bent his head and charged. He crashed into the line, just off center. Head down, feet churning the turf, he plowed through the Washington line. Then, like a locomotive, he began gathering steam. He plunged through the secondary, bowling defenders aside like tenpins, and headed straight for the safety man.

Disdaining finesse, Nagurski bent his red neck and charged ahead under full steam. The collision between him and the safety man could be heard all through the ball park. With no one between him and the goal line, Nagurski kept going, head bowed, till he had crossed the goal line, bounced into a goal post, bounced off, knees jerking, kept on another 30 yards and then crashed head on into the concrete side of the baseball dugout.

A few seconds later, Bronko staggered up the steps of the dugout, still clutching the ball.

"Wow," he muttered painfully when he got back to the Bears' bench—"that last guy sure hit me hard!"

Norm Van Brocklin, one of the great college and pro quarterbacks turned coach, was telling some of his Atlanta Falcons about his days at the University of Oregon.

Oregon was playing USC one Saturday afternoon, and Norm was getting his lumps from one particular savage lineman. Every time this big fellow dumped him, he managed to give Norm an elbow or a fist in the face.

Finally, a battered and bleeding Van Brocklin complained to the Ducks' captain. "What am I gonna do with this guy?" Norm said. "He's killing me!"

"Tell you what," said the captain. "Let's teach this guy a lesson. Let's take advantage of him. I'll tip off the ref to what's happening. Then, when we're in a tough third-down spot, we'll let this guy slip in on you. When he gets close, you call him a dirty name. He's bound to slug you, and we get the penalty and a first down. How about it," he said to Van Brocklin, "you willing to take one more crack in the jaw for dear old Oregon?"

Norm sighed, "Okay, anything for dear old alma mater."

Oregon lined up shortly afterward, with a third-and-nine situation at the midfield stripe. They needed that first down badly for ball possession. This was the time for Van Brocklin's sacrifice.

The pass was called. The big lineman was allowed to slip in. As he charged at Van Brocklin, Norm threw the ball in desperation and hissed, "You dirty so-and-so!"

When in Doubt, Punt!

Bang! The lineman let Norm have one right in the face.

When he came to a few moments later, he saw the Ducks' captain leaning over him.

"Well, how about it," Norm said weakly, "did we get the penalty call all right?"

"Well, um, you see," the captain said, "the pass was complete for a touchdown, so naturally we declined the penalty!"

Another Vince Lombardi story is related by Carroll Dale, about the time the late coach of the Packers was handed a high-priced and big-headed collegiate halfback. Lombardi could suffer almost anything but inattention to football—especially when he was lecturing.

It was the morning of a big game against the Giants, and Lombardi was going through a brief rerun of the game plan. Suddenly he noticed that the rookie back was sitting in a corner, reading a comic book.

"You!" he barked. "Bring that thing here!"

The rookie rose sheepishly and brought Lombardi the book. Vince looked at it a moment, handed it back and said, quietly, "That's all. Go back and sit down."

The young halfback was delighted. He figured that his reputation had caused Lombardi to go easy on him. He sat down and resumed reading.

The veteran Packers weren't that easily put off by Lombardi's mild manner. They knew his scathing tongue all too well. They waited for the storm.

The game began, and at the half the score stood 14–14. The young halfback hadn't seen any action yet, and he chafed impatiently on the bench, anxious to show the stuff that had made him an All-American in college.

Finally, midway through the third period, with the game still deadlocked, Lombardi called his name. "Warm up!" the coach shouted.

The kid jumped up and began running up and down the sidelines, doing deep knee bends, flexing his muscles, grandstanding for all he was worth. After a couple of minutes, Lombardi beckoned to him.

"Ready?" Lombardi asked.

"You bet," said the halfback.

"Good," said Lombardi, handing him a comic book. "Then start reading!"

Bear Bryant's reputation at Alabama has been based on the teams and players he's coached (Joe Namath was one of Bear's boys) rather than his witticisms, but quarterback Scott Hunter tells of his sophomore year at Alabama, when Bryant came up with a good one.

Alabama was playing Tennessee and the Vols were pushing hard for a touchdown early in the first period.

On a second and three the Vols quarterback faked a handoff, then threw deep to his split end. The pass was completed; the end twisted away from two defenders, and only a safety stood between him and the goal line.

The end scampered along the sideline. The Alabama defender closed in for an easy shot, but the nimble-footed receiver practically faked him out of his shoes, got past him and scored.

A few moments later the safety disgustedly trotted to the bench, shaking his head. He flung his helmet on the ground."Oh, what an idiot I am!" he muttered. "What a dope! What a stupid, dumb cluck!"

Bear Bryant stood up and patted him on the shoulder. "Sit down and be quiet, son," he said. "Nobody's arguing with you!"

College coaches like Bryant, Charles McLendon, Jack Swarthout and Bob Devaney help make pro football the great game it is today by nursing along young athletes. Then there was Peahead Walker of Wake Forest fame. Walker put his heart and soul into coaching little Wake Forest. One season, most of his energy and love was being spent on a star running back, who was, unfortunately, injury-prone.

As long as this 190-pound gazelle was in the game, Wake Forest did splendidly. But each Saturday, like clockwork, he was knocked out of the game and carted off the field.

Midway through the season, Peahead was getting desperate. Came a big game, and, with the help of the team trainer, Peahead taped and padded his star, stuck him in protective harness and sent him out to do or die for dear old Wake Forest.

As luck would have it, on the first play from scrimmage, the star running back had his number called. He took the handoff and hit the right side of the line. A hole opened for a fraction of a second—then closed like a nutcracker on the luckless runner. The sound of the crunch could be heard in the stands.

When the bodies were shoved aside by the linesman, the back lay stretched out, cold as a side of beef in a butcher's locker. Frantically Peahead rushed in from the bench, the team doctor in his wake.

As they bent over their stricken warrior, Peahead said, "You got to fix him up, Doc. He's got to play or we're done for!"

The doctor shook his head. "Not so fast," he said. "I'm not even sure yet the poor kid's breathing."

"So what!" yelled the agitated coach. What kind of doctor are you! *Make* him breathe!"

One of the great pep-talkers among college coaches was Mike Murphy, who was at Penn years ago. Mike, who for years had been waging a courageous fight against tuberculosis, had a standard act he used every season.

When in Doubt, Punt!

He waited for the biggest, the toughest, the most important game; then, before the game, he gave his spiel.

Came the Big Game this particular season, and Mike, as usual, shambled slowly into the locker room, cleared his throat painfully, coughed a hacking cough and began to speak in a hoarse, strained voice.

"Boys," he barely whispered, "this is probably the last game I'll be coaching. Maybe the last game I'll ever see. But I don't care, honest I don't. If I can just see my boys win just once more, well, I'll go to meet my Maker a happy man. So don't let Old Mike down today. Let him die with the memory of seeing Penn win. Let today's victory be Old Mike's epitaph!"

A sophomore back who had never heard the speech before turned to a senior. Tears were in his eyes. "Gee," he said, "I never realized. I sure hope Mike can stay on till the end of the game."

"Don't bawl, kid," said the senior dryly. "I've heard this for three years straight now. If you ask me, Old Mike'll outlive all of us!"

One of the most hypnotic pieces of pregame oratory ever recorded was given by Fielding "Hurry-Up" Yost. The coach must have had something going for him, because over a 25-year span his Michigan team won 169 while losing only ten.

Yost was indeed a genius as a coach, and a Svengali

145

of the locker room. One day, his usual fiery pep talk was even more eloquent than usual. The players sat in the dressing room absolutely entranced. At last, Yost reached the grand climax of his oratory.

"Go out that door!" he screamed, his voice filled with the thunder of a backwoods preacher, "go out that door," he repeated, waving his arms wildly, "go out that door to VICTORY!"

His obedient players, stirred by emotion, mesmerized by his voice, blinded by tears of rage, sprang up as one man and, with an animal roar, stampeded furiously through the door the coach indicated—and into the swimming pool.

Yost had pointed to the wrong door. Six fully clad and near-drowning players had to be fished out of the water before order was restored.

The college coach's job is often a thankless one. When his boys lose, irate alumni and fans yell for his scalp. Nobody loves a losing coach—but nobody.

Take the case of Harry Stuhldreher. In the midst of the clamor to get him fired as coach of Wisconsin some time ago, an irate alumnus wrote to a Madison newspaper suggesting a couple of out-of-town high school coaches to replace the former Notre Dame star.

The angriest reader of the item was young Skippy Stuhldreher, oldest of Harry's sons and himself the star quarterback of the Madison West High School 11. He sat down to write a stinging letter of protest to the paper. Harry stopped him.

"Don't do that," he staid. "Part of my job as coach is taking abuse, and part of your job as my son is taking it with me."

"I will not," snapped Skippy. "If they want a high school coach to replace you they should get mine! He's the best man for the job!"

Among the many problems facing college coaches is the one of a player's eligibility. Football stars who chronically fail exams give coaches gray hair, and so it's understandable when a harassed coach makes excuses for some of his less bright charges.

Jim Plunkett says this story took place at Stanford. It could be—and in any case, it might have happened at any university.

The Stanford coach was called in by the dean, shortly after midsemester exams, affecting the eligibility of certain players.

"This is serious," said the dean. "You know how we feel about cheating. Well, a couple of your boys taking the same examination came up with the exact same answers on nine out of ten questions. How do you explain that?"

"Well," sputtered the coach, thinking quickly, "those

are two of my smartest boys. I guess they studied together and memorized the same answers."

The dean nodded. "I thought of that possibility. But it's the answer to one particular question that bothers me."

"How so?" asked the coach.

"See for yourself," replied the dean. He handed the exam papers to the coach. To one of the questions, the first player had answered, "Don't know."

The other had written, "Neither do I."

In a game as rough as football, Bob Harrington of Detroit University proved to be a very unusual fellow. He played through four years of high school and four years of college without so much as suffering a scratch. Eight years of bone-bruising football action and not a mark to show for it.

And now Bob was in the last game of his college career. Detroit was playing Villanova. Gus Dorais, coach of Detroit watched Bob play from the opening whistle until five minutes before the end of the game, then decided to bring him off the field, ostensibly for a rest but really to give the fans a chance to accord Bob a well-deserved ovation.

Unmarked as usual, Harrington trotted off the field, the cheers of the fans following him. He flopped on the bench next to coach Dorais. On the next play, Detroit swung an end sweep toward their own bench. The Detroit ball carrier was flung bodily into his own teammates, right where Bob was sitting. A horde of Villanova defenders rode his back.

When the tangle was unscrambled, there was poor Bob stretched out flat. Kicked in the face, he had lost two teeth, one eye was turning purple and his cheek was cut. He was aroused by liberal dashes of cold water. At last, Bob opened his eyes and looked into the anxious face of Dorais.

"Please, coach," he said, through battered lips, "let me back in the game, where it's safe!"

Gene Washington, the peerless pass catcher, was talking about his days playing high school football. His 11 was having a bad season, and on one particular Saturday they were being murdered. Down by four touchdowns in the last few minutes of the game, all they cared about was getting back to the locker room in one piece.

They got possession, and the quarterback called the huddle. "A-36," he snapped. "Fullback takes it through right guard."

"Please," said the fullback. "Not me. I can't run. They almost broke my leg last time."

"Okay. C-24. Halfback on the sweep to left."

"No!" groaned the halfback. "Last time we tried that I lost a tooth, not to mention five yards!"

"All right, then," the quarterback said in despair. "I'll take it up the middle myself."

"No!" cried the center. "Those linebackers are jamming the middle. They'll kill me!"

At this point the referee paced off five yards for too much time. Again the quarterback called the huddle.

"Okay," he said, "any of you guys got any bright ideas?"

"Yeah, me," said Washington. "How about a nice long incomplete pass?"

The violence of football, college or pro, has led to some strange stories and even stranger fantasies. Writer Wells Twombly tells about the spiritual medium from Oakland who kept phoning the local sports desk, saying she had a spirit message for quarterback John Brodie. One Sunday night, a weary editor said to her, "Okay, who's the message from?"

"From Pappy Waldorf," the woman said.

"It can't be," said the editor. "Pappy Waldorf is still alive."

"Well then," the medium said, "maybe it's *for* Pappy, *from* John Brodie. They hit him pretty hard out there this afternoon, you know."

When Buck Buchanan, the great defensive tackle, played in college, he was used on offense as well. For

When in Doubt, Punt!

a while, at least. Until one important game, when his gargantuan bulk proved of more help to the other side than his own team.

The time was late in the fourth period, and Buck's boys were leading, 14–13, toward the end of a grueling afternoon. Then, deep in his territory, the quarterback called for a punt. The ball was snapped and the ball was kicked, but somehow Buck got his assignment messed up, and his huge bulk suddenly appeared in front of the punter, just as the ball took off.

The pigskin smacked Buck square in the seat of the pants, bounded high in the air behind the kicker and was gleefully grabbed off by the defensive end. Without any- one's laying a hand on him, the man ran the last few yards into the end zone for the game-winning touchdown.

As Buck trotted gingerly into the bench, waiting for the lightning to strike, his coach walked over to him and said, quietly, "How do you feel, my boy?"

Surprised and grateful, having expected a storm of abuse, Buck smiled. "I'm fine, coach," he said, rubbing the seat of his pants, where he had been struck.

"That's good," said the coach, sweetly. "I was afraid you might have gotten a concussion of the brain!"

What with playful undergraduates planting time bombs on gridirons and painting enemy campuses with red paint, the following incident may seem a trifle tame.

151

Between the halves of a game between Cornell and Colgate, not long ago, the Cornell band marched out on the field, played a few home team tunes, then followed the drum major over to the Colgate side. There, in true sportsmanlike tradition, the musicians began shifting around preparing to spell out something for the Colgate fans.

When the word was finally formed, however, it spelled out: P E P S O D E N T.

When Len Dawson first joined the Steelers, he didn't seem to get along with coach Buddy Parker. Len was kept on the sidelines by Parker, and for a long time didn't get to see a second's action in a game. As a star at Purdue and a first round draft choice, Len quite naturally smarted under this treatment.

Then, one midweek afternoon, during a "skull session," Parker drew a situation on the blackboard and suddenly snapped, "Okay, Dawson, what would you do in this spot?"

"Me?" said Len, surprised. "Why I'd just rub a little more resin on my pants so I wouldn't slide off the bench."

When Bobby Bell began playing football for his high school team, in Shelby, North Carolina, their game was six-man football. It was a hard game, and big Bobby played safety on defense, quarterback on offense.

When in Doubt, Punt!

There was one game, he recalls, when his team was taking a fearful shellacking from a bigger and tougher team. Bobby and his mates were bruised, battered and on the wrong end of a something like 40–0 score in the fourth quarter. Bobby took over at that point, called a pass play, took the snap, then fumbled. The ball squirted out of his hands, took a couple of crazy bounces and landed right in front of a teammate.

The wary youngster looked up just in time to see three big bruisers from the other side bearing down on him. He hesitated.

"Pick up the ball!" yelled Bell. "Pick it up!"

"Not me," said his teammate—"I didn't drop it!"

Bell remembers that in those days he played for a pick-up sand-lot team as well, and, with not much money to go around, the boys just managed to raise enough for 11 uniforms. The subs on the bench wore old clothes.

In practice one day before a game, the regular full-back was hurt, and was taken away in an ambulance to a nearby hospital. Bell and another player jumped on their bicycles and pedaled furiously after the ambulance.

Arriving at the hospital, they insisted on seeing their teammate, who was being treated in the emergency room. When they were admitted, the examining doctor said to them, "Well, it's nice to see his friends are so worried about him."

"Oh, we're not worried," said Bell. "We just came to get his uniform!"

Red Friesell once refereed a game between the convicts and guards of a penitentiary. Late in the game, the star fullback of the convict team broke away and ran down the field toward what looked like a sure touchdown. Friesell followed the play as fast as he could and blew his whistle as the convict reached what Red thought to be the goal line. The runner slowed down as he heard the whistle and was brought down by a pursuing guard, and only then did Friesell realize that he had blown the whistle too soon—at the ten-yard line!

The referee was embarrassed. "I'm sorry," he said to the disappointed convict. "I'm really sorry. I just made a mistake."

"Don't let it get you," said the convict. "Up here we've all made mistakes."

Finally, a tale about one of the greatest football players, and indeed one of the all-time super athletes in American sports history—Jim Thorpe.

Some time ago, there were two rival townships in the Midwest which were always at each other's throats. Each boasted that it was a better town than the other in every way. Never was this rivalry more intense than when the annual football game was played between the two teams representing them.

One year, a prominent citizen of one town decided to play a trick on the other by bringing in a "ringer" to play for his team. His choice was Jim Thorpe. The citizen persuaded Jim to go along with his hoax, and then on the big day sat back to watch his team win.

But as the two teams trotted onto the field to begin the game, it occurred suddenly to Jim that he didn't know any of the team's plays or signals. Grabbing the quarterback, he explained the situation.

"You're right," the man agreed, "but what can we do now?"

"Tell you what," said the famous Carlisle Indian, "whenever you want me to carry the ball, just slip me a little wink and let me worry about the rest."

As soon as his team got possession, the quarterback began feeding big Jim the ball. But every time he carried the pigskin, Jim found that he was running up the backs of his own interference and getting nowhere. Disgusted, the great star called time.

"Listen," he growled in the huddle, "you guys gotta get out of my way. Now when that ball is snapped and you hear me give a yell, all you guys on the left side of the line head toward the left sideline. All you guys on the right side of the line head for the right sideline. The center, as soon as he's passed the ball—he falls down flat on his face."

The quarterback gulped at this amazing set of instructions, then said, "But Jim, what about us in the backfield?"

Jim looked wearily at his three backfield mates. "Well," he said finally, "you're my interference, aren't you? When you hear me yell—follow me!"

BASKETS, BIRDIES
and BODY CHECKS

Pete Maravich, the dynamic guard of the Atlanta Hawks, came to the NBA with a tremendous amount of fanfare. A three-time All-American at LSU, Pete nevertheless recalls one of his less glorious games at State. He missed shot after shot, and finally, in the third quarter, he was taken out.

Angry at himself, he pleaded with the coach. "Don't take me out," he said. "We're losing. We need shooters out there."

"Not shooters," said the coach. "Scorers!"

Superstar Cazzie Russell was explaining at a basketball clinic how he prepared himself for a game.

"I do a few dozen knee bends, a couple dozen pushups, run around the gym a few dozen times and go through 15 minutes of shooting drill."

Then it was Dick Barnett's turn to face the audience. Someone asked "Tricky Dick" how *he* warmed up for a game.

He replied, "All I have to do is watch Caz warm up and I'm already bushed!"

Sonny Hertzberg and Red Auerbach, historical names in New York and Boston respectively, were arguing one day about the merits of pivot men they'd seen down through the years. After discussing the talents of today's giants, they went back to the days of the "little men."

Said Sonny, "The best six-three pivot I ever saw was Tom Ferrick."

"Frank Ramsey was better," claimed Auerbach. "When Frank missed a shot, he followed up and got the ball right back for you."

"Very nice," said Sonny. "But Ferrick didn't have to get the ball back. He never missed!"

Hot Rod Hundley likes to tell how it was playing basketball around West Virginia. Sometimes, playing against a small town college on its home grounds, it was almost impossible to win. "You had to beat the 'homer' refs as well as the team," recalls Rod, going on to relate the following classic dialogue, which took place in a badly lit gymnasium, late in the game.

"I can't see the scoreboard," said Rod to the referee. "How much time we got left, and what's the score?"

"There's just 50 seconds left to play," said the referee, "and *we're* ahead by four points."

By and large basketball refs are astute, hard-working officials whose proximity to the seats makes them easy targets for jibes and complaints from the crowd.

Lou Eisenstein, a great official, was working in Boston one night when he detected a player crowding an opponent trying to take the ball out along the end line.

"Give him three feet," called out Lou.

From the crowd came a partisan voice, "Quiet, Eisenstein, or we'll give you *six* feet!"

It's been many years since the great CCNY basketball teams of Nat Holman excited the fans at the old Madison Square Garden. A favorite Beaver strategy in those days of ball-handling basketball was the "freeze," in which the team that was ahead would pass the ball around and keep possession as long as possible before taking the shot.

It was beautifully executed and beautiful to watch. But for fans of the losing team, as well as the losers themselves, it was very frustrating.

In the closing minutes of one game against NYU, the Beavers started their freeze. Finally, Al Roth took a pass just outside the circle and poised, looking up at the basket a long moment.

Came a voice from the Violet's side of the Garden, "Shoot, Roth—you got the wind with you!"

College as well as pro basketball has speeded up considerably since then, with the accent on scoring rather than ball handling. But back when there was still debate in college basketball about a 24-second possession limit, Placido Gomez, coaching little Brooklyn College, said as far as he was concerned, such limits made no difference.

"Right now," he said, "my boys can't even hold on to the ball for *ten* seconds!"

The shooting game has also changed in basketball with the advent of big and still bigger men. The name of the game is getting your big man in there to dump the ball in. Set shooting, from far out, is not so highly regarded. But the long shot is beautiful to behold, and one of the longest shooters in the game used to be Bob Schafer of Villanova.

Once, after a Seton Hall–Villanova game, coach Honey Russell of Seton Hall was asked if Schafer had been taking any really long shots.

"Long?" exclaimed Russell. " We were playing in Philadelphia and he was shooting from Pittsburgh!"

The amiable priests at Seton Hall have long held a reputation as basketball fans. But few of them actually understood the game, as much as they enjoyed watching it played. The story goes that an Archbishop once came to Seton Hall on a visit, and was invited to watch the Pirates play that evening.

He sat in the stands among the priests, and, after watching the Pirates fall behind in the first half, he said to the priest next to him, "It seems Mr. Russell will have to be using strategy very soon."

"Strategy?" said the priest, consulting his program. "What number is he?"

The great Bob Cousy didn't have many technicals called on him in his career. But one time, he remembered, Sid Borgia called one on him and then, after the game, came over and said, "Bob, would you mind autographing a program for my neighbor's kid?"

Cousy sighed. "So you want my autograph, eh? A few minutes ago it cost me $25 just to speak to you!"

Basketball programs are usually dull, prosaic affairs, written with little imagination. Some years ago, however, the programs at Fort Wayne bore the imprint of a genius with a sense of humor. Among the tintypes of the players, were these:

Corky Devlin, of the Atlantic City Devlins. A family

of great restraint. Corky lived there all his life and never once entered a Miss America contest.

Larry Foust, an easy man to keep track of in crowds. He's a pivot man. Never turns around, always pivots. He has several shots—tetanus, typhoid, etc.

Trainer Stan Kenworthy: The players don't call him "doc" for nothing. He pays them. When we don't have any injuries, he usually trips someone. This is known in his trade as job security.

One of the classic pregame pep talks in basketball annals was given by Ken Loeffler, coaching little LaSalle against rich, mighty Princeton. In the locker room, just before the two teams were to meet in the NCAA quarter-finals, Loeffler said:

"Men, next door is a bunch of apple-cheeked young athletes. Their fathers own the factories you'll be all working in the rest of your lives. This will be your last chance to get the better of them."

Final score: LaSalle 73, Princeton 46.

Hockey, too, has its humorious moments among the flashes of skates and sticks. It is a rough, bruising game. Once, during a particularly tense, brawling contest, little Camille Henry, one of the tiniest players in the NHL, lost his temper and tangled with big Fernie Flaman, a much-feared slugger.

As they grappled on the ice, little Henry suddenly shouted a warning to Flaman, who outweighed him by a good 50 pounds: "Watch out, Fernie, or I'll bleed all over you!"

Another tough hombre was Steve Buzinski, a Rangers goalie. Once Buzinski was knocked down in front of the net and lay there bleeding, apparently unconscious. A crowd of players and officials gathered around him.

"Somebody should get five minutes in the penalty box!" shouted one Ranger. "They knocked Steve down with their sticks!"

"Liar!" came back from a Red Wings player. "He got hit by the puck!"

"He got hit by a stick!" said the Rangers.

"By the puck!" shouted the Red Wings.

At this point Buzinski raised himself on an elbow, glared around him, and said, "Like heck it was the puck, I got hit by a stick!"

Then he closed his eyes and quickly lay down on the ice again.

The Rangers' Phil Watson was a fiery spirit, both as a player and as a coach. Once, after losing a tough game, he was surrounded by reporters in the locker room. But before anyone could open his mouth, Watson, still seething about the loss, declared, "I have nothing to say, nothing! Now, any questions?"

Watson was a tenacious scout of young players. Once, he heard about a hot prospect from Montreal whose family didn't think too much of the home-town Canadiens. Digging deeper into the situation, Watson found that the prospect doted on his seven-year-old brother. So, at Christmas, Phil sent the lad a bright-red sweater with the letter "R" emblazoned on it—a not too subtle hint.

The next morning the youngster came downstairs and, unwrapping his presents, came across the sweater.

"Look what I got!" he exclaimed. "One of Rocket Richard's sweaters!"

Babe Pratt, the old Rangers defenseman, tells this story about his son Tracy, who was up for a trial with the Chicago Black Hawks.

In the office of general manager Tommy Ivan, Tracy was sounding off just a bit.

"How good am I?" he said. "I don't like to brag, but I can shoot like Bobby Hull, stick-handle like Stan Mikita and make plays like Pierre Pilote."

"Then you must be pretty good," smiled Ivan.

"My only problem," admitted Tracy, "is that I lie a little."

That tale brings to mind the anecdote about the tall-story-telling fisherman who went on a vacation to Maine.

After three weeks of lolling about, he got on one of the local buses and entered into a conversation with a stranger.

"Like it up here, do you?" said the stranger.

"Terrific!" said the fisherman. "Listen, it may be out of season, but I've been catching the biggest rock bass I ever saw in my life. Been pulling giants out of the lake. Oh, by the way, who are you, stranger?"

"I'm the local game warden," came the reply. "Who are you, mister?"

The fisherman gulped and said, "I tell you warden, I'm just about the biggest liar in this whole United States!"

Lies, of a different kind, are very much a part of the game of golf.

Arnold Palmer, one of the all-time greats, tells of the golfer he once knew who became notorious for sneaking his ball into a better playing position, called a "lie."

When the man suddenly died, all his golf club members joined in the arrangements for his funeral. Then the president of the golf club instructed the funeral director:

"Make sure you stamp the ground down hard after he's lowered into the grave."

"Why?" asked the puzzled undertaker.

"Because if you don't, he'll be trying to improve his lie."

Golfers have the reputation of being the most insane addicts of the game. Nothing stops a golfer from his rounds. Golf "widows" abound, wives whose husbands are forever disappearing on the links on weekends, not to appear again until darkness forces them home.

Bobby Nichols' favorite story of the obsessed golfer who *had* to play 18 holes every Sunday goes like this:

One particular Sunday the man, call him Mr. Jones, left early in the morning as usual to play with his regular partner, Charley Smith. He told his wife he'd play just 18 holes and be back home by four in the afternoon.

He finally appeared again on his doorstep at seven that evening, looking absolutely exhausted.

"What a day, what a day," he moaned to his wife.

"How about me!" she shrieked. "You said you'd be home at four, and look what time it is!"

"You don't understand," Jones said. "Charley and I were on the third green this morning when suddenly he keeled over and died of a heart attack!"

"How terrible!" cried his wife. Then she said, "But then, where have you been till seven o'clock!"

"Well," explained Jones, "the rest of the afternoon, it was—hit the ball and drag Charley, hit the ball and drag Charley . . ."

Another story in the same vein was told by Doug Sanders at a Walker Cup dinner.

The golfing foursome are waiting to tee off when, alongside the course, a funeral cortege goes by.

One of the foursome doffs his cap and holds it over his breast in respect.

"Did you know the deceased?" asks one of the four.

"Yes," replied the man sorrowfully. "We would have been married 20 years tomorrow."

Comedian Bob Hope is one of the mad golfing fraternity. Once, he recalls, he was obliged to play with a club guest, a film director from England. The man fancied himself a golfer, but kept getting sixes and sevens, hitting the ball into the woods and traps.

Finally, on the 14th hole, the man turned on his caddy in a rage.

"You useless little blighter!" he roared. "What good are you? Not once have you opened your silly mouth. Not once have you advised me what clubs to use or shots to play on a strange course."

The caddy regarded the Englishman silently.

"Just once, just once," the man continued, "tell me what to use!"

"You want to know what to use, mister?" the caddy said. "Use an old ball, a real old ball!"

Novice golfers are fit subjects for laughs. They can look awkward until they get the hang of the game, and their naïveté can be wondrous.

Here's a small selection from Dow Finsterwald:

The golf pro took his star pupil up to his first tee. He pointed to the distant green and said, "Now hit the ball as close to that flag as you can."

The duffer took a mighty swing and, as luck would have it, reached the green just two feet from the cup."

"What do I do next?" he asked the pro.

"Knock it into the hole," the pro explained.

"Into the hole?" said the beginner. "Why didn't you say so in the first place!"

The beginning golfer stepped up on the tee and took his first swing ever at a golf ball. The shot landed on the green and trickled right into the cup for a hole in one. The other three members of his foursome were struck dumb. On the second hole the beginner stepped up and did it again—another hole in one!

"Gosh," he said to his awed partners, "that was close!"

"Close?" said one, "what do you mean, close?"

"Why," answered the beginner, "I almost missed that time!"

Golfers are so intent on good scores that even when nothing is at stake in a game—usually the case—they will cheat and lie to get their strokes down. Thus this story about the two hackers slashing their way around the course one day. After the first hole, the fellow marking down the score asked, "How many strokes did you take?"

"Five," came the answer.

"My hole then," said the scorer. "I got a four."

On the second hole the question was of course repeated, and the first man said, "Six."

"My hole again," said the scorer, "I got a five."

Came the third hole. Both men holed out, and the scorer asked, "How many?"

"Oh no," said his friend, "this time it's my turn to ask first!"

The golfer sliced his tee shot into the woods. His opponent, waiting nearby on the fairway, heard him take two shots before he got back on. "How many so far?" he asked.

"That's two," the man replied.

"But I heard you take two in the woods," said the other.

"Oh, that first one was just a practice swing."

His opponent thought a moment and said, "Well, okay; I'll take your word, but that's the first time I ever heard anybody cursing out a ball on a practice shot."

Chi Chi Rodriguez, explaining away his putting miseries during a recent tournament: "I read the greens in Spanish, but I putt in English."

Golfers concentrate so hard on the game they become oblivious to everything around them. For example, there is the story of the golf fiend who returned home after a hard day on the course. His wife kissed him and remarked that their son, John, had just come in as well. "He says he's been caddying for you," she said.

"Say, no wonder the kid looked so familiar!" exclaimed the golfer.

And there's the story that comes from Mickey Mantle, an avid golfer himself. Mickey tells the one about the golf club secretary who one day saw a man taking practice swings on the 18th green, using a niblick. Naturally, big chunks of green were in danger. Sure enough, as the secretary rushed up, he was hit in the face by a huge divot —that mixture of earth and greenery usually dug up by golfers on the less sensitive fairway.

Sputtering, the secretary raged, "Hey, you—what's wrong with you?"

The niblick-swinger replied, "I dunno, I think maybe I'm dropping my left shoulder too much."

A little girl was watching in fascination one day as a desperate golfer was trying to get his ball out of the rough. After hacking away for a while, he gave up in disgust.

The little girl turned to her mother. "That man has stopped beating it, Mother, so whatever it was, it must be dead."

Joe Louis, one of the great heavyweight boxing champs of all time, succumbed to the golfing bug, and in fact became quite good at the game. During World War II, holding the rank of sergeant, he managed to find off-duty time to play golf with an old crony of the links, Porky Oliver, a top pro. Oliver was a corporal.

Louis liked to play for money. Since Oliver was not adverse to adding to his meager corporal's pay, he agreed, and soon was separating Louis from hundreds of dollars. But one day Louis announced, "We're playing for double or nothing today, and you're spotting me eight strokes."

Oliver protested. Joe pointed to his stripes and said. "I'm pulling rank."

After collecting his money at the end of the day, Louis seemed conscience-stricken. Deadpan, he said to the crestfallen Oliver, "Tell you what. I'll give you a chance to get even. Let's go up to the gym and box four rounds. I'll spot you the first two."

The late Craig Wood was one of golf's funniest men. He was a great storyteller. One of his favorites was of the time he was driving toward New York with fellow pro Vic Ghezzi. Wood had just won the New Jersey Open at Pine Valley, then considered among the world's toughest courses. Wood turned on the car radio just in time to hear Orson Welles's famous broadcast of *War of the Worlds*, which described an invasion of the Earth by Martians so realistically that it actually panicked thousands of listeners. Wood stopped the car and listened for a few minutes. Then he turned to Ghezzi and said, "Just my luck. I finally break par at Pine Valley, and the world comes to an end."

Reporter to lady golf pro Clifford Ann Creed: "Clifford sure is a funny name for a girl." Miss Creed's reply: "Why? I've got a brother named Alice."

Though boxing is considered by some to be less than a gentlemanly sport, it does have its lighter side. Muhammad Ali (Cassius Clay) is a talented joker outside the ring, but his skill doesn't match that of some of the old-time word-jabbers.

Take "Slapsie Maxie" Rosenbloom for example. Slapsie, once a lightheavyweight champ, got to be so funny that he appeared in comedy roles in several films. He was a genuine ad-libber, too. Once, in a Broadway restaurant, a discussion was going on about sportsmanship inside the ring. Someone asked Maxie, "Do you really hate your opponent?"

Replied Maxie, "He's hittin' me, ain't he?"

Joe Louis, for all the deadpan expression that was his trademark, had a dry sense of humor. Just before his bout with Two-Ton Tony Galento, Joe was being lectured by his trainer, Jack Blackburn, about the advisability of taking a count after a knockdown.

"I know you're proud and don't like to be seen on the canvas," said Jack, "but if you get knocked down stay down till nine."

Joe nodded. But during the fight, Galento caught him with a left hook and sent him sprawling. Before the referee could even begin his count, Joe was on his feet again. At the end of the round, Blackburn scolded him.

"I thought I told you to take the nine count," he said. "Why didn't you?"

Deadpanned Joe: "Why let him get all that rest?"

Louis was a fabulous champion. Many a hopeful fighter ended his career on the canvas against the famous Brown Bomber, as he was known then. Max Baer, who held the title himself at one time, was due to face Louis one autumn. He spent the summer at a beach resort, training. A bit of a joker himself, Max told everybody he was trying to get a good tan so that in the ring nobody could tell him and Louis apart.

"They'll be able to tell you apart all right," someone said. "The one standing up will be Louis."

Among the classic remarks coming *after* a fight with Louis was the one uttered by Jack Roper. After being knocked out in the first round, Roper mumbled into the microphone: "I zigged when I should have zagged."

And then, after that Baer–Louis fight, came this exchange between the two Maxie's—Baer and Rosenbloom. Rosenbloom was ribbing Baer about the licking he'd taken, and Baer replied, "Kid me all you like, but you must admit that for a while there I gave Louis a good scare."

"You sure did," agreed Rosenbloom. "For a while there he must have thought he'd killed you!"

Judging a fight is difficult, and often the judges' decisions reflect this difficulty to the point of being ludicrous. Take, for example, the decision after the Kid Gavilan–Paddy Young fight some years ago. The opinions of the three judges were as far apart as Nixon's and Mao's. Referee Conn called the bout a draw. Judge Agnello gave the fight to Gavilan, six rounds to four. But Judge Susskind ruled in favor of Gavilan nine rounds to one.

When the decision was announced, somebody boomed down from the balcony, "Hey Susskind, who spoiled the no-hitter?"

Kingfish Levinsky was a fighter who provoked laughter inside as well as outside the ring. Once he toured England, where he delighted the natives with his manhandling of the English language.

At the end of the tour his new friends gave a banquet in his honor. When the guests were seated, the host rose to his feet for the traditional English toast. All the others rose, except the Kingfish.

The host raised his glass. "To the King!" he proclaimed.

"To the King!" echoed the rest.

At this point Levinsky rose to his feet, smiling.

"Gee, fellas," he said—"thanks a million!"

Then there was the time Levinsky was training for a fight in Chicago. He woke up one morning, put on his shoes and tried to walk. He fell flat on his face.

"Get me a doctor!" he cried. "I've gone lame!"

Quickly the trainers called in a physician.

"It's me feet, they hoits," said Kingfish. "What's wrong with me?"

The doctor took a quick look. "It's your head, not your feet," he said. "You've put your shoes on backwards!"

There was one fighter who had taken a couple of punches too many. He began to be troubled with insomnia. He went to the doctor, complaining that he could get no sleep.

"Try counting sheep," the doctor advised.

Two weeks later the fighter was back, desperate.

"Did you take my advice?" the doctor inquired.

"I did," said the fighter. "I tried counting sheep. But every time I got to nine I jumped up and started swinging."

Another fighter, similarly afflicted with several fights too many, kept asking his manager to get him a certain match. "Get me Blinky Smith, get me Blinky Smith," the fighter nagged. "I can beat him!"

The manager kept insisting the match couldn't be made.

"Why not? Why not? I want to fight Blinky Smith!"

Finally the manager gave it to him straight. "I can't get you a match with Blinky Smith," he said, "because *you're* Blinky Smith!"

When Joe Frazier trains for a fight, he looks as savage as he does when actually in the ring. Sparring partners aren't always the easiest to find. One day, when he was training for his fight against Ali, he was pounding away at the big bag. Into the gym walked a strong-enough-looking boy, and manager Yank Durham said to him, "How'd you like to box a round or two with Joe? I'll give you $25."

The young man took a look at what Joe was doing to the punching bag and said, "No thanks. I already got $25."

Sugar Ray Robinson was considered by many boxing observers to be the best fighter, pound for pound, of all time. He held world championships in several divisions. He was also a smart businessman, and knew what he could command at the box office. But he was realistic about it, too. Thus, one day, he was skeptical when some promoters began offering him ridiculous guarantees for a nationwide exhibition tour.

"What would you think," said one of them, "if you woke up tomorrow, put on your pants and found $100,000 in your pocket?"

"I'd think," replied Ray, "that I'd put on somebody else's pants."

Some people believe that bull fighting is an even crueler sport than boxing. When Sidney Franklin was at his height as a bull fighter, he was cornered at a party one evening by a lady who began insulting him for taking part in the sport.

Courteously, Sidney tried to give his side of the story. But the woman wouldn't let him get a word in. She kept up a steady stream of abuse.

Finally, Sidney got his chance to speak. "Madame," he said, "it is true I have killed many bulls in the ring. But you may sure of this: Never would I be so cruel as to bore them to death."

The sports world has accelerated as the pace of life in general has become quicker. The accent is on speed, whatever the sport.

In track, this is easily measurable. The once-formidable challenge of the four-minute mile is just a memory now. All the good long-distance runners break four minutes. But when Finland's Paavo Nurmi set the mile mark at 4:10.4 in Sweden several decades ago, it was considered such a fabulous achievement that word of the record was flashed all over the world.

In America, track fans could hardly believe it. One excited university track star burst into his philosophy classroom upon hearing the news and announced it. "Sir," he said to the Professor, "Nurmi has just knocked two seconds off the mile record! Two seconds!"

The professor looked at him over the rims of his spectacles. "Very interesting," he said. "And what does the gentleman plan to do with the time he has saved?"

Gil Dodds, known as the Flying Parson, was an ordained minister at the time he was becoming famous as America's greatest miler.

One night, after a big victory, he was asked by a reporter to explain his terrific time in the race.

"The Lord ran with me," said Dodds sincerely.

The same reporter then turned to the runner-up, who

had been badly outdistanced. "And what happened to you?" he asked.

"Well, I had to run alone," he muttered.

In a recent European track meet, a Hungarian hammer thrower easily beat the competition. Asked about his victory, he said, "It is easy for me to throw the hammer so far." Then he added, in an undertone:

"And I could throw it still farther if I could throw the sickle with it!"

The babel of languages in international track-and-field competitions often causes confusion. There was the Hungarian female javelin thrower who was being interviewed by American newsmen. One said, "Ask her what she likes to do in her spare time back home?"

After going through several translations, the report came back, "She says her brother's name is Bela and he is a student at the university."

Television has had so much impact on sports that its effects are really immeasurable. Youngsters, even those who may never have seen a contest except on television, have become quite sophisticated about every sport. Which brings up the story of the eight-year-old who was finally taken to see his first real live basketball game.

"Look!" he exclaimed to his father when the teams came out to warm up. "It's in color!"

From the Knick's Walt Frazier comes this story: The family was grouped around the television set watching the Knicks play the Celtics one night—relatives, neighbors' kids, the lot. Then somebody began shouting out at the bad play of one of the Knicks. "Look at him, he's all left feet, he can't make a shot, he not covering his man —why don't they take him out of the game?"

"Well," said a six-year-old visitor, "maybe it's his ball."

Willie Reed and Greg Fillmore were arguing the merits of an enemy center one night, and Reed said, "You got to admit that at least he's a steady player."

"Steady?" exclaimed Fillmore. "That's his trouble. If he were any steadier he'd be motionless!"

The name of George Mikan rings many a memory bell in the minds of basketball fans. In his time he was the highest-paid basketball player in the pros. But when he first came up to De Paul to begin his college career, he was only a tall, gangling youth with little but his great height to recommend him. The freshman coach to whom he first reported sized up the skyscraper.

"You got a uniform?" he asked.

"Everything but shoes," said the shy young Mikan.

"I'll get you a pair," said the coach. "What size?"

"Fifteen or 16," said George. Then he blushed with embarrassment. "Make it 15, huh, coach," he said. "I don't want to look conspicuous."

Pep-talk stories are popular in all sports, Most of them relate how, in one way or another, a coach fired up his boys so that they went out and on to victory.

This one is a little different.

When Lew Alcindor was at UCLA, the Bruins had one of the smaller West Coast colleges on its schedule more for tradition than for competition. On the night of the annual game, Alcindor and company were not exactly exerting themselves to roll up the score.

During the half-time, the Bruins were taking the break in their dressing room. Next door, separated by just a thin partition, was the other team. The Bruins could hear the enemy coach giving his boys a pep talk, and he was coming on loud and strong.

"You gonna let them swell-head Hollywood blowhards lick you like this?" they heard him rant. "You gonna get beat by a bunch of press clippings?" On and on went the coach, turning the air purple with his name-calling of the UCLA players.

Finally, he wound up his tirade, saying, "Now go on out there and beat those bums!"

Whatever the effect on his own players, there was no

question about the effect his pep talk had on the Bruins. They charged out for the second half and gave the little college the worst beating they experienced in all their history!

Meanwhile, back on the fairway, Bob Hope and Bing Crosby were playing an exhibition golf match for a national charity. Naturally, both played dead-serious golf, as serious as those two could ever get about anything when working together.

On the ninth hole, both landed on the green on the second stroke. Crosby's ball was two feet from the cup. When the two friends reached the green followed by a tremendous crowd, Bing went into his act. He measured the distance to the cup, went down on all fours to study the lie, checked the wind and then turned gravely to his caddy.

"When was this green mowed last?" he asked.

"This morning, sir," the lad replied with a grin.

With Hope grumbling and muttering in the background, Bing continued his reconnoitering of the hole. Then, apparently satisfied, he stepped back, lined up the shot and dropped the ball neatly into the cup.

"Very nice," sneered Hope. "Naturally, you'll concede my shot?"

"Not a chance, needle-nose," replied Crosby. "You got an 18-inch putt there. Take your best shot, man!"

Hope went through the same routine as Bing. Then he turned to the caddy. "You sure this green was mowed this morning?" he asked.

"Oh yes, sir," the boy said.

With this assurance Hope lined up his shot, stroked the ball gently and watched it roll right past the hole. The crowd let out a howl of amusement, with Bing laughing louder than the rest.

Drawing himself up to his full height, and looking down in contempt at Bing's caddy, Hope said, icily, "What time this morning?"

Then there were the two good friends who were anything but good friends on the golf course. It's just that kind of game. Still, fair weather or foul, the two men played an 18-hole match every Sunday—for blood. The matches were played strictly according to the rules of golf, with but one exception. It was agreed between them that either player could tee up the ball if it landed on the fairway.

One Sunday they came up to the 18th and final hole all even. Each drove off the tee, up and over a long rise. As they walked down the fairway together, they saw that one ball had landed squarely in the middle, the other in a slight depression just at the edge of the fairway. The first player ambled toward that ball, at the same time taking a tee from the holder in his golf cap.

"Hey, wait just a minute!" yelled his friend, "that ball's in the rough, not on the fairway!"

"Really?" said the first man. "It looked to me like it was on the fairway all right."

"It's in the rough!" growled the other.

"I still say it's on the fairway," said the first golfer.

"I say it's on the rough and it can't be teed up!" insisted his friend.

The first player sighed. "Well, I won't argue," he said. "You say it's on the rough, eh?"

"Right!"

"Can't tee up, eh?"

"Right!"

"Okay," said the first player. "Then go ahead and play it, because it's your ball!"

Golf, exasperating game that it can be, brings out the temper of many an otherwise mild-mannered man. In fact, mutterings, oaths and swearing have become almost standard equipment among the weekend regulars of the golf world.

Once, Arnold Palmer agreed to give some lessons to an esteemed member of the United States Senate, a man known for his dignity of bearing. Taking him out to a course near the capital, Arnie showed him a few basics, and then suggested they try nine holes, so that the Senator could get the feel of actual play.

The two men teed up for the first hole. Palmer hit first, to give further demonstration of proper position and stroke, then stood aside for the Senator. The gentleman took his place, swung mightily and succeeded in uprooting several square inches of dirt. The ball, however, remained untouched.

Again the Senator took a swing, and again he jammed the clubhead into the turf behind the ball.

He swung a third time. A huge cloud of dust filled the air. When it cleared, it appeared that the Senator had been more successful this time; the ball lay about a foot in front of the tee.

The Senator glared at the ball and muttered something under his breath.

"Did you say something, sir?" asked Palmer.

"I said 'Tut-tut,'" replied the dignified member of Congress.

Palmer shook his head sadly. "Sir," he said, "you'll never learn golf with those words!"

To wind up a book of sports stories, what is better than a story *about* one of the greatest sports story spinners of all time—the late Damon Runyon. His beat was largely the worlds of horse racing and boxing, but he loved everything that had anything to do with sports. And everybody who had anything to do with the sports world loved Damon.

For several years before he passed away, Runyon was

deprived of the use of his voice. Despite the handicap, he never wavered in his interest in sports, and although he couldn't speak, he would carry on an argument with the use of a pad he carried.

One night he was having a discussion with his close friend Eddie Walker, the fight manager. While Eddie voiced his opinions, Damon would scribble his on the pad. The subject got around to the relative abilities of Henry Armstrong, a champion of the day, and Joe Gans, one of the old-time champs.

Walker was carrying on about Armstrong, about how great he was, how hard he could hit, how well he could box and so forth. At the same time, he was putting down Joe Gans. Runyon, defending Gans, was scribbling his remarks rapidly on the pad and passing them across to Walker.

The argument got hotter and hotter, with Runyon scribbling ever more rapidly and furiously. Finally Walker tried to close out the discussion.

"Not only would Armstrong have stopped Gans," he said, "but he would have done it inside three rounds!"

The angry Runyon grabbed his pencil again and almost snapped it in two as he outlined in big bold capital letters the word NO. And after the two letters he stabbed a four-inch tall exclamation point into the paper.

Walker read his friend's comment, and then looked at Runyon with a wounded expression.

"Okay, okay," he said, "but you don't have to yell at me!"

The words "and in conclusion" bring to mind the after-dinner speaker. And thus, in conclusion, an afterdinner-speaker sports story.

Red Patterson, the Dodgers vice-president, has made so many afterdinner speeches recently that one night, when his wife banged two dishes together in the sink, he got up and spoke for 15 minutes on the glories of Richie Allen.

Milton J. Shapiro says about himself:

"I was born and raised in the Canarsie section of Brooklyn, in the days when every corner had its sandlot and its sandlot sports, from baseball to the vanishing art of marbles. At P.S. 115 and Boys High School, I played at all sports, excelling at none, but from my earliest years I was sports minded and enjoyed playing at any game wherever I could. After high school I entered the Baruch School of Business at the City College of New York, intending to major in economics, but the war interrupted my education and changed my thinking. I spent two years in the Air Force, part of it in the South Pacific, where I managed to find time for more sports, playing on basketball and football teams with the 13th Air Force.

"In the army I first thought of writing as a career. On my return to civilian life, I re-entered City College as an advertising major, worked on *Ticker,* the undergraduate newspaper, as a feature columnist and editor, and while still a senior I got a job as copy boy on a New York newspaper. On graduation I was promoted to the sports department, then switched to the entertainment desk as movie critic. From newspaper work, I moved on to free-lance writing, magazine editing, was sports editor of the *National Enquirer* and executive editor of a magazine company. I am now a free-lance writer specializing in sports books for young people."